THE LEADERSHIP STYLE OF JESUS

THE
LEADERSHIP STYLE OF JESUS

MICHAEL YOUSSEF

This book is designed for your personal reading pleasure and profit. It is also designed for group study. A Leader's Guide with helps and hints for teachers and with visual aids (Victor Multiuse Transparency Masters) is available from your local bookstore or from the publisher.

VICTOR BOOKS
A DIVISION OF SCRIPTURE PRESS PUBLICATIONS INC.
USA CANADA ENGLAND

Second printing, 1986

Most Scripture taken from *The New King James Version.*
© 1979, 1980, 1982, Thomas Nelson, Inc., Publishers. Used by permission.
Other quotations are from the *Good News Bible* (GNB): © American Bible
Society 1966, 1971, 1976. Used by permission.

Recommended Dewey Decimal Classification: 301.155
   Suggested Subject Heading: LEADERSHIP: EXECUTIVE ABILITY

Library of Congress Catalog Card Number: 85-63318
ISBN: 0-89693-168-4

© 1986 by SP Publications, Inc. All rights reserved
Printed in the United States of America

CONTENTS

76551

To
Elizabeth
Sarah
Natasha
Joshua
and Jonathan

my partners

1 *Part*

THE BEGINNINGS OF LEADERSHIP

CHAPTER ONE

THE NEED TO BE CONFIRMED

A pastor friend preached a children's sermon while wearing a specially made T-shirt under his robe. Suddenly he announced, "I have something to tell you—something I've never told anyone before in my life!" He tore his robe open, revealing the T-shirt, and declared, "I am Superman!"

The children laughed. Finally one child called out, "If you're Superman, fly up to the ceiling!"

The pastor proceeded to explain that many people make claims about who they are. "The problem is that once I tell you I'm Superman, I have to prove it," he said.

Leadership works that way too. When people announce their leadership, they need to prove that claim. They need the backing of others who will say, "Yes, this person *is* a leader."

Even Jesus had to prove Himself before others followed Him. Once a few recognized Him as the promised Messiah, they became witnesses and confirmed His messiahship.

John's Gospel shows that Jesus offered repeated confirmation of His claims. He pointed not primarily to His miracles, but toward more basic proofs. At least seven different confirmations of Christ's ministry can be found in this Gospel; after we've examined them, we'll tackle the question of how they apply to leadership in today's churches, businesses, and other organizations.

First Witness: The Father

God the Father Himself sent Jesus Christ as Saviour of the world. Our Lord told His hearers, "And the Father Himself, who sent Me, has testified of Me" (John 5:37).

The Father's stamp of approval was not given in secret. It pleased God to confirm Jesus' leadership publicly, right after Jesus was baptized by John.

At that moment, "Behold, the heavens were opened to Him and He [Jesus] saw the Spirit of God descending like a dove and alighting upon Him; and suddenly, a voice came from heaven, saying, 'This is My beloved Son, in whom I am well pleased'" (Matt. 3:16-17).

Thus in the presence of John and others who came for baptism, the Father openly announced to the world the bond between Himself and Christ. What a contrast with Muhammad, the founder and prophet of Islam, who secretly entered Jerusalem at night and claimed to hear the voice of God speak to him alone! What a contrast with others who seem to boast of their special ministries which began when, "In the middle of the night, God awakened me and spoke to me."

Jesus did not have to tell the world by Himself that He had the right to be a leader. The Father openly concurred.

On a less public occasion, Jesus took His three closest disciples to the place later known as the Mount of the Transfiguration (Mark 9:2-8). There they saw further confirmation as Christ talked with Moses and Elijah.

Christ was no self-proclaimed leader. He began with the greatest of witnesses—and He did not stop there.

Second Witness: John the Baptist

John baptized Jesus and saw the Spirit descend like a dove. As Jesus said of him, "He has bore witness to the truth. Yet I do not receive testimony from man; but I say these things that you may be saved" (John 5:33).

The "voice crying in the wilderness" had also confirmed Jesus' credentials when he met the Lord near Bethany. Seeing Jesus coming toward him, he said,

> Behold! The Lamb of God who takes away the sin of the world! This is He of whom I said, "After me comes a Man who is preferred before me, for He was before me." I did not know Him; but that He should be revealed to Israel, therefore I came baptizing with water (John 1:29-33).

John the Baptist was not only a forerunner. He was a man aware of his unique ministry—to confirm the identity of Jesus Christ to the world.

Third Witness: Christ Himself

It may seem strange at first that Jesus called Himself a confirmer of His own ministry. But after referring to His Father and John the Baptist, He added, "I have a greater witness than John's" (John 5:36).

On another occasion He said, "I and My Father are One" (John 10:30). His hearers understood perfectly and attempted to stone Him, "because You, being a Man, make Yourself God" (v. 33). Later He said that if people had seen Him, they had seen the Father (John 14:7).

Christ didn't merely *claim* to have a unique relationship

with God. Everything about His life backed it up. Without gimmicks, tricks, or promises to make His followers wealthy and powerful, He made it clear that He was a leader to be followed.

Fourth Witness: The Spirit

As already noted, the Holy Spirit gave His blessing at Jesus' baptism by descending on Jesus. He also remained on Him (John 1:34).

While we may not fully understand what happened because of the symbolism of the language, it certainly tells us that the Spirit of God confirmed the ministry and leadership of Jesus Christ. The presence of the Holy Spirit gave Jesus the authority with which He spoke and performed miracles (Matt. 7:29; Mark 1:22, 27; Luke 4:36).

Fifth Witness: Scripture

The Old Testament confirmed the ministry of Jesus. Prophets foretold His coming, His ministry, and His death. Isaiah especially pictured His birth (Isa. 9:6); His suffering (53:4-10); His servanthood (42:1-4); and even that one would come first to announce Him (40:3).

Jesus told the Jewish leaders who argued with Him, "You search the Scriptures, because in them you think you have eternal life; and these are they which testify of Me. But you are not willing to come to Me that you may have life" (John 5:39-40).

Sixth Witness: Miracles

Jesus' ministry confirmed *itself* through the miracles He performed. John's Gospel refers to them as "signs." Though he cites fewer than any of the other Gospel writers, those he mentions bear witness to Jesus' purpose and power.

Christ did not perform these signs as acts of showmanship, however. No egotist would have performed some of His most outstanding miracles away from the crowds, often telling those He healed not to tell others. The healing of the man at the pool (John 5) or the man born blind (John 9), for example, seem to have had only a few eyewitnesses. This fact confirms His words, "I do not receive honor from men" (5:41).

Seventh Witness: The Disciples
The disciples traveled with Jesus throughout His earthly ministry. They saw what He did, heard His teachings, and believed. When religious leaders began to persecute the Lord, and He spoke openly of the hardship of following Him, many would-be disciples turned away—but not all.

Those who stayed with Christ, including Peter, said, "You have the words of eternal life" (John 6:68). Peter didn't mean only that Jesus knew the rules or the way of life, but that He was the giver of life eternal. And the Apostle John closes his Gospel by saying that he is bearing witness to—confirming—the life and ministry of Jesus (21:24).

Today's Leaders
We who enter leadership today hardly do so wtih the unique qualifications of Jesus Christ. But we can learn this principle from His life: *The call to leadership must be confirmed.*

What would we think if, in the middle of a worship service, a stranger walked to the pulpit and said, "I am come to lead you into truth?" Aside from the strangeness of the approach, how would we know who he was? How would we know that he was right?

We'd ask one question quickly enough: "By what right (or authority) do you speak?" We might not say it quite that way, but confirmation would be one of the first things we would demand.

Most denominations have set up orderly ways to ordain or otherwise recognize leaders. They realize that while people may *train* for leadership, only God *calls.* The church acts as a confirming agency. This process often begins when people grow into leadership roles in a local congregation and members recognize their uniqueness.

The church board and titular head of the congregation may confirm it when such people announce their intentions for ministry. If the denomination has educational requirements, its school confirms the call as well.

Spiritual leaders are even to be "confirmed" in a sense by those outside the church as well. The Apostle Paul, instructing Timothy on the subject of ordination, says the leader-to-be "must have a good testimony among those who are outside lest he fall into reproach and the snare of the devil" (1 Tim. 3:7).

The rule of confirmation applies to *any* kind of leadership. In business, church, home, and other settings, people must *earn* the right to lead. I may believe I have been divinely appointed to head one of the world's great corporations, for example, but who would hire me if I walked into the main office of Nestle's or Shell and announced, "I am here to take over"?

I would have to prove my ability, perhaps starting "at the bottom." Like many leaders, I might rise to the top in a company after beginning in an entry-level position. I would need initiative and skill to move up, and some person or some group to stand behind me at each upward step, saying yes.

Yet some people try to go "straight to the top" in and out of church. I've seen would-be executives and candidates for ordination who vainly insisted they had what it took to do the job. One candidate for ministry, when turned down, accused the examining committee of "going against God." The committee was made up of his friends, all of whom wanted to confirm what he claimed to be God's call. But they couldn't. They saw too many character flaws in the man.

I've even hired some executives who came with all the "credentials' but proved totally unable to lead. They had neither the aptitude nor the confirmation of others. I've since learned to spot such pretenders in the interview stage; the first sign comes when the candidate tells you how he will save your organization, that the institution is desperate for someone with his ability. That "red light" signals that the person is not a confirmed leader.

And so we come to the first leadership principle to be learned from the life of Jesus:

PRINCIPLE 1:
JESUS RECEIVED CONFIRMATION BEFORE HE COULD LEAD. SO MUST WE.

CHAPTER TWO

ACKNOWLEDGING THOSE WHO HAVE GONE BEFORE

At an artists' awards banquet the first honoree spent several minutes thanking people who had helped him earn his award—teachers, family, friends, and fourteen members of an artist's group to which he belonged.

When the second winner came to the podium to accept a trophy, however, his speech was short: "I thank you for your judgment in giving me this award. I also want to tell you that I did it by myself!"

The second man was joking—but his words remind us of many in leadership positions today. If they achieve results, they take the credit. Even if they don't put it into words, they think, *I earned this all by myself.*

But they're wrong. None of us achieves anything alone. We've all been influenced or helped by others.

Giants of the Past
Sir Isaac Newton said, "If I have seen farther than other men, it is because I have stood on the shoulders of giants."

He acknowledged those who had pioneered the way for him. He earned the "Father of Physics" title, but didn't do it alone.

I'll always remember something one of my professors said. When you do research, he instructed, keep searching until you notice one or two names that keep coming up as references. Those one or two people probably laid the groundwork in that field. Others built on their foundation or tried to build their own in opposition. Even the opposition had to acknowledge the original.

That's a characteristic of good leadership. It admits its accomplishments honestly and sincerely—and says, "I couldn't have done it alone."

My Acknowledgments

I, for instance, have an earned Ph.D. To get that far I received help from many people. First, I owe my Christian faith to godly upbringing by my mother, who prayed for and with me earnestly.

At age twenty-one I emigrated from Egypt to Sydney, Australia. I was a stranger in Sydney, knowing only one couple—and them only by name. But I also had a letter of introduction to Anglican Canon D.W.B. Robinson, later Archbishop of Sydney. It was through the encouragement and support of Archbishop Robinson that I overcame the hurdle of being unable to communicate effectively in English; in fact, without his encouragement I wouldn't have been able to study at Moore Theological College.

Then I met John Haggai, who had faith in me. He asked me to head the Haggai Institute, a worldwide ministry with offices on six continents. Doing so helped me to grow to what seemed like fifty years' worth of maturity—in eight years. With God's help, I was able to lead this organization, study for my doctorate, and write books—all at the same time.

All the while I had a most trusting partner: my wife Elizabeth, who gave me love, support, and encouragement. She mothered—and fathered—our four children as I traveled overseas or stayed up late to study.

By standing on the shoulders of the aforementioned "giants," I felt there was nothing I couldn't do. I owe so much to these four people and to many others. I could never forget or deny their impact on my life and ministry.

Biblical Forerunners

Jesus told His disciples that the fields were ready to harvest, obviously using this as a symbol of spiritual readiness. He added,

> He who reaps receives wages, and gathers fruit for eternal life, that both he who sows and he who reaps may rejoice together. For in this the saying is true: "One sows and another reaps." I sent you to reap that for which you have not labored; others have labored, and you have entered into their labors (John 4:36-38).

Jesus wanted His disciples to know that they owed a debt of gratitude to those who had labored before them. He could easily have reminded them that the very land they stood on had been won in combat by Joshua and the faithful Israelites. He could have mentioned the rabbis and other leaders who kept the Jewish faith and taught the people.

When the Apostle Paul wrote to the Corinthians, he had a similar idea in mind. The Corinthians had begun to elevate the leaders they liked and align themselves with them.

> Who then is Paul, and who is Apollos, but ministers through whom you believed, as the Lord gave to each one? I planted,

Apollos watered, but God gave the increase. So then neither he who plants is anything, nor he who waters, but God who gives the increase. Now he who plants and he who waters are one, and each will receive his own reward according to his own labor. For we are God's fellow workers (1 Cor. 3:5-9).

Jesus came to His own ministry, but only after John the Baptist had prepared the way. Peter owed his connection with Jesus to his brother Andrew, who invited him to follow the Lord too. And the Book of Acts implies that the martyrdom of Stephen had a powerful effect on Paul, which helped make way for his conversion.

Interdependence

Why did Jesus, after training His followers, send them out by twos? (Luke 10:1) Having a second person along obviously would encourage a traveler in a strange place. But I wonder whether Jesus had an additional reason in mind.

Might Peter have come back after visiting a city all by himself, saying, "Look what I did"? Could it be that from the start Jesus wanted His followers to see their dependence on one another—and on their Lord? He may even have wanted to prepare them for the "one body in Christ" idea. Later Paul's writings would constantly call the church back to that concept (Rom. 12:3-8; 1 Cor. 12:12).

Jesus Himself could have taken credit for everything from Creation onward. But He acknowledged the rules of the faithful, readily pointing to Abraham as the father of the Hebrew nation, for example (John 8:53).

Had some of *us* come as Saviour of the world, we would likely have discredited those who had gone before. We might have said something like, "Moses was a good man, all right, but he got angry and disobeyed. God had to punish him. Good old Abraham did a lot of fine things, but he had weak moments. Why, one time he feared Pharaoh so much that he said Sarah was his sister! But I'm different. . . .

How to Acknowledge Others

If we want to follow Jesus Christ as leaders, we must acknowledge others in a Christlike way. Remembering the following facts may help:

1. *Every ability is God's gift.* John the Baptist said it best: "A man can receive nothing unless it has been given to him from heaven" (John 3:27). He knew that he did not send himself as the Lord's forerunner; God had endowed him. Realizing that we have leadership ability only because God gave it humbles us.

When the Apostle Paul wrote about spiritual gifts (1 Cor. 12), he used the same principle. No matter what gifts the Corinthians had, they all came from God. They did not invent gifts, nor could they bestow them on themselves.

2. *We did nothing to earn our leadership abilities.* One doesn't earn a gift. It's a matter of grace, not merit, when one is given the ability to lead.

3. *This gift gives us no cause for boasting.* God gives one person leadership ability, another the talent to recognize and follow good leaders. Some people have gifted hands; others are especially articulate or can think more deeply than their peers. But none has reason to brag about having received a gift.

4. *We should acknowledge those who helped us sharpen our abilities.* Olympic athletes begin with outstanding talent; but even for them that is not enough. They need help, instruction, correction. A weight lifter needs a coach to teach him how to breathe properly; a runner needs to be told when she is pointing her toes slightly to the side, costing her precious seconds in competition.

Leaders are the same way. I know *I* needed help along the way. Someone saw a glint of leadership aptitude in me and encouraged it; others taught me additional lessons.

5. *We should give thanks to God for our abilities.* Since I know my capacity to lead did not originate with me, I can pause regularly and thank God for making me as He did.

A writer friend makes thanksgiving for his gifts part of his prayers every day. He says something like this: "Thank You, Lord, for making me a writer. Help me to be the best writer I can be with the talent You've given me."

This friend knows he must work to improve on his talent. During his childhood he read anything given to him, gradually learning to distinguish good writing from poor and superior from mediocre. When he eventually began to write, he leaned on the lessons he'd learned through years of poring over the classical writers.

With such an attitude, he acknowledges God who gave the initial ability—and the giants on whose shoulders he stands.

PRINCIPLE 2:
LEADERS ACKNOWLEDGE THE GIANTS
WHO PRECEDE THEM.

---

2 Part

THE QUALITIES OF LEADERSHIP

CHAPTER THREE

THE LEADER AS SHEPHERD

I'd just finished having lunch with Bob Guyton, the chief executive officer of a large banking institution. As we walked out of the bank's executive dining room, we passed a suite of offices. The banker paused to say hello to the receptionist there, asking about her husband, whom he knew had been hospitalized. Later, when we got off the elevator, he greeted by name two bank employees who were waiting there Finally, at the front of the bank, he called the guard by name and asked about the man's wife—also by name.

Hundreds of people must have worked in that big bank, yet that top official knew the name of every one! I walked away amazed, not so much that he had a good memory, but that he actually knew those names. He knew not just the executives, but the supposed "nobodies." From his comments I could guess that he knew more than their names; he knew them as persons, individuals with different personalities and problems.

I remember thinking that Bob was a "good shepherd" of sorts. Jesus said, "I am the Good Shepherd; and I know My sheep, and am known by My own. As the Father knows Me, even so I know the Father; and I lay down My life for the sheep" (John 10:14-15).

Knowing the Sheep

That busy executive knew his "sheep." He evidenced honest concern for them and their families. I'd long known of this leader's business acumen, but that incident gave me a whole new appreciation for him.

By contrast, another incident showed me a different kind of "shepherd." One Sunday I stood next to the pastor of a prestigious church at the conclusion of the service. He shook hands with every parishioner, heartily greeting them with a bright smile and a cheery, "How are you?"

In at least a dozen instances the pastor said, "Ah, that's good," before the person could even reply. Then his hand would go out to the next in line with the same smile and the same greeting. When one elderly woman reached the pastor, he said, "I hope you're doing well today."

The short, sad-faced lady answered quickly: 'My husband got sick in the middle of the night Thursday and I finally called an ambulance. He's still in the intensive care unit at. . . ."

"Yes, so nice to see you this morning," the pastor said blithely. "Always a joy to have you in the service." Immediately his hand went out to the next person in line.

I could hardly believe what I'd heard. I felt embarrassed because the pastor did not listen, shocked that he behaved so insensitively, and hurt for the woman's sake. In a fumbling way I tried to make up for it, though as a visitor I didn't want to get too involved. "What's your husband's name?" I asked the lady. "I'd like to remember him in prayer every day next week."

I don't mean to judge that pastor. I can understand that with a congregation of well over 2,000 people, an over-worked staff, and the heavy load he carries, he probably did not know every person in line. He may have been burdened with personal problems that day, or anxious about an up-coming event. But I left the church with an impression quite different from the one given me by the banker.

The banker knew his sheep. The pastor—and *pastor* is another word for *shepherd*—did not know his. Worse, I felt he didn't seem to care about not knowing them.

When Jesus talked of His relationship with His sheep, He gave the impression of knowing much more than their names. For Jesus, knowing them meant loving them.

Loveless Shepherds?

Loveless hearts can't know the sheep. Loveless shepherds view sheep as numbers in the registry, members on the books, employees on the payroll, statistics about which to boast.

Here's how these shepherds might refer to their sheep:
- "We had a 20 percent increase in membership this year."
- "We have more employees and do twice as much business as our nearest competitor."
- "Surveys indicate that 83 percent of all Canadians recognize our product."

We live in a society that places its highest emphasis on numbers. TV programming rises or falls on the size of the viewing audience; people judge a local church's merits by its size; a company succeeds if its bottom line shows an increase over the previous report.

As a result, good TV programming comes in second to ratings. For the church, teaching, fellowship, and worship often don't seem as important as membership totals. And the quality of a company's products and service take a backseat to profits.

The Jesus Style

Statistics don't stack up to the leadership style of Jesus. He knows His sheep intimately. His love for the sheep is not an abstract idea, nor can it be replaced with a cliché such as, "I love my people." His love for the sheep, while collective, is still individualized; He knows His flock because He knows each member.

How do Jesus' sheep know Him? Not by chance, not by intellect alone, not by understanding certain truths about His leadership—but by sensing the love of the Shepherd directed toward them. As a sheep, I may doubt and fear; but when I see the Leader, the Shepherd, my doubts and fears melt away. I respond to the affection and concern of the Shepherd.

Consider the shepherds and sheep of Jesus' day. Shepherds in Palestine put the safety of their sheep before their own; in the Old Testament, for example, David fought and killed a lion with his bare hands because the predator tried to attack his sheep. By understanding this deep commitment of shepherds for their flocks, we gain more insight into the metaphor Jesus used in calling Himself a Shepherd.

The Good Shepherd placed the needs of His sheep first; even going to the extreme of pouring out His life for them. Jesus quoted Zechariah 13:7 when He predicted His death to His disciples. He said, "All of you will be made to stumble because of Me this night, for it is written, 'I will strike the Shepherd, and the sheep of the flock will be scattered'" (Matt. 26:31). Ironically, the smiting of the Good Shepherd insured the safety of His sheep. He willingly gave His life for His own.

That brings us to another principle drawn from the leadership style of Jesus:

PRINCIPLE 3:
GOOD SHEPHERDS KNOW THEIR SHEEP; GOOD LEADERS KNOW THEIR FOLLOWERS.

If that sounds strange to us, it's probably because most of us think of a leader as the person at the start of the line, the senior statesman, the great general, the head of the parade—somewhat aloof from his followers. Taking the "lead" is one aspect of leadership, but true shepherds are also serving, self-giving.

Jesus Christ calls leaders to serve, though most of us prefer to lead and let the sheep follow if they choose. While He calls us servants, we prefer to give orders.

Shepherds Keep Moving

Wise shepherds constantly lead toward greener pastures and better opportunities. They take their sheep toward the still waters, where turbulence, pressures, and factions don't disrupt. But not all shepherds lead wisely.

Take one of the largest retail chain stores in the United States for example. It used to rank near the top, but fell largely because it did not keep abreast of changing times. The leaders of its main competitor, however, carefully studied customers' upward economic mobility and upgraded their stores. That second chain has remained strong, even diversifying its activities; now they deal in banking, real estate, and insurance as well as retail and all of those operations are successful.

The leaders of that second chain succeeded by being "with-it." In the jargon of business, that means being up-to-date, knowledgeable, alert to changes, sensitive to people's needs.

As the true shepherd keeps his flock moving, he is both "with-it" and "with-us." One of the titles of Jesus is *Emmanuel,* meaning "God with us." That reminds us that as He leads, He never leaves nor forsakes us, no matter how difficult the road we travel.

The real task of leaders for today is to combine those qualities. We need that touch of intimacy, while also saying, "We're moving ahead."

Jesus' final words to His followers contain both qualities. He sent them out by saying, "Go therefore and make disciples of all the nations, baptizing them in the name of the Father and of the Son and of the Holy Spirit, teaching them to observe all things that I have commanded you; and lo, I am with you always, even to the end of the age" (Matt. 28:19-20). They would be moving on—and He would be going with them.

The Risk of Moving On

Jesus had a plan of action. He never intended for His followers to remain huddled in a small group in Jerusalem. Yet they either didn't understand His Great Commission or didn't want to obey it right away. As the Book of Acts records, the disciples stayed around Jerusalem. They might have been content to remain there forever; but the Good Shepherd wouldn't allow His flock to languish in a small corner of the Middle East. Luke says "At that time a great persecution arose against the church which was at Jerusalem; and they were all scattered throughout the regions of Judea and Samaria" (Acts 8:1).

The apostles might never have moved out and taken risks unless Jesus Christ allowed the persecution to push them out. Once they moved, the faith spread all over the civilized world; by A.D. 325, Christianity had become the official religion of the Roman Empire.

Translate that concept into the business or church world, and the leadership style of Jesus mandates taking risks. The leader stands before his followers, employees, stockholders, church members, and sees the potential in a new idea. He says, "Let's do it."

The Visionary Shepherd

In the mid-1970s a young pharmaceutical salesman named Stan worked with doctors and hospitals to set up health seminars for the public. Years later Stan's idea became standard practice in many American hospitals.

But Stan had another idea—preventive medicine. He came up with a brilliant plan to work with corporations to encourage their employees to prevent illness. His research indicated that employees missed many days of work every year, at a financial loss to their companies, and that many of those absentee-days could be eliminated.

His flexible program would offer incentives for people to lose weight and exercise. It would cost the corporations money, but he could show how they would save in the long run.

Stan talked with over 700 corporations about his idea. But not one of them would take the risk! They gave varied reasons which boiled down to not seeing the value of the program. Yet by the early 1980s large corporations had begun to accept the concept of preventive medicine.

Stan's dilemma is common to visionary leaders. They have the ability to look ahead; to imagine things the "sheep" would have to see to believe. They can predict turns in the roads, detours, and diversions. Sometimes they have to forge ahead whether others see or not. The pivotal verse in Luke's Gospel reads this way: "Now it came to pass, when the time had come for Him to be received up, that He steadfastly set His face to go to Jerusalem" (Luke 9:51). As recorded in succeeding verses, the disciples didn't understand. They were busy thinking about sending fire to burn up a village. Jesus looked ahead to Calvary.

While leaders need visionary qualities, they need to be careful not to walk too far ahead. Shepherds, even those "with a vision," must have the welfare of their flocks at heart. I can think of nothing worse than to hear church members say of their visionary but overly ambitious pastor, "He's building his own little kingdom."

Empire building is dangerous. One of the firms that first built computers went bankrupt because it overextended itself. One of the company's sales representatives later said, "He [the inventor and president] wanted to be the biggest, but didn't care about being the best. He didn't care when employees quit because he thought he could always hire somebody else just as good."

Balanced Shepherding

In whatever field we find ourselves as leaders, we need the quality of being *with* our coworkers, employees, parishioners, or family members so they sense that we care about them. We can't be everyone's best friend, but we can be available and open to people.

The president of a large fast-food restaurant chain for instance, has an open-door policy. "Anybody in the company can come to see me at any time," he says, and his employees know that. He's a busy man, but not too busy to listen. His company, in an industry whose managerial turnover runs as high as 50 percent *annually,* has less than a 5 percent annual turnover rate!

Yet faithful leaders also balance their relationships with others so that they can push these followers onward. Most people want to rest awhile, to remain comfortable where they are. Once they get used to a lifestyle, they don't want to stretch or try new things. The effective leader constantly says, "Forward! March!"

Jesus knew how to maintain this balance. On the one hand, He promised the disciples they would have His presence and comfort through the Holy Spirit. But He also turned their eyes beyond an obscure city in the Middle East to encompass the world. Luke records His words which incorporated both principles:

> But you shall receive power when the Holy Spirit has come upon you; and you shall be witnesses to Me in Jerusalem, and in all Judea and Samaria, and to the end of the earth (Acts 1:8).

What Makes a Good Shepherd?

Growing up in the Middle East, I was able to observe firsthand the tender relationship between the sheep and the shepherd. In Western culture we have to travel a long distance to see sheep, and even when we do our mass farming practices don't help us explain this vivid image Jesus used to explain His leadership style.

For the shepherd, the reward comes in seeing that his sheep are contented, well fed, safe, and flourishing. His energies are spent not just to make a reputation for himself, but rather to supply the sheep with the finest grazing in the lushest pasture, to store winter feed, to find clear water. Good shepherds spare no effort in providing a shelter from the storm. They constantly watch for ruthless enemies, diseases, and parasites to which sheep are so susceptible.

From dawn to dusk these good shepherds selflessly dedicate their days to the welfare of their woolly followers. They do not even rest during the night; they sleep with one eye and both ears open, ready to leap and protect their own at the slightest sound of trouble.

When Jesus claims to be the Good Shepherd, He is not just another leader. Many of the religious leaders of His day claimed to be shepherds of Israel, but Jesus saw their hypocrisy, self-centeredness, inability to lead, and failure to protect their flocks. Jesus was saying, in effect, "I am the Shepherd *par excellence.*"

"In My leadership," Jesus is saying, "you will find guardianship, companionship, sustenance." All responsibility is laid on His broad shoulders, and all tenderness in His deep heart. There is no aloofness or coldness. His sheep will not have an associate shepherd return a phone call. He is the Good Shepherd. Loving the sheep is His style.

CHAPTER FOUR

COURAGE

Muhammad's followers today number millions across the world, with Islam one of the fastest-growing religions. Yet in the beginning he had few converts. Almost no one understood him. In his writings he poured out his heart about the blessedness of finding a soul who would believe in him. He promised multiplied blessings on those first converts for believing and following him.

There have been many leaders, religious and secular, who seemed ready to bribe their first converts. By "bribe" I mean to pay with promised blessings or favors or the feeling that they are special. That's a fairly average way to start any kind of movement, business, or other activity. Leaders work hard to get the first ones and thoroughly enthuse them, so that the movement generates its own growth.

By contrast, Jesus made no great promises at the beginning of His ministry. All the biblical record mentions Him saying while recruiting is, "Follow Me" (John 1:43).

Even more surprising, Jesus did not cultivate the influential to promote His cause. John records the story of

Nicodemus coming at night to visit Jesus. He describes Nicodemus as "a man of the Pharisees. . .a ruler of the Jews" (John 3:1). We can infer from those words that Nicodemus was of the Jewish hierarchy. Mention of the Pharisees, a religious order of the most conservative type with a name that means the "separated ones," tells readers that no ordinary man of the people came to Jesus.

Think how flattering it would have been if Nicodemus had become an early convert! Jesus could have boasted, "I have disciples in high places." Isn't it strange that Jesus offered Nicodemus no greater welcome than He did anybody else? He held out no inducements or promises; He met him without offering a word of praise or affirmation that recognized the man's status.

Jesus listened to the smooth words of Nicodemus: "Rabbi, we know that You are a teacher come from God; for no one can do these signs that You do unless God is with him" (John 3:2).

When Nicodemus paused, Jesus did not say, "You are on the right track. Just keep on doing your best." The presence of a ruler of the Jews did not intimidate the Lord. He did not say what many Christian leaders say today when they talk to non-Christians, particularly to those who come from other religions such as Buddhism, Hinduism, or Islam: "You have part of the truth and we have part of the truth, and we are all struggling together."

Jesus faced that highly trained religious leader head-on by telling him, "You must be born again." He didn't give Nicodemus the words he wanted to hear; He didn't commend him for coming or for listening; He didn't try to influence him to join with the other disciples. Instead He violated all the rules of good selling by confronting Nicodemus with a spiritual requirement.

No Compromise

By the standard of many leaders today, Jesus made one of the dumbest mistakes possible when He talked with Nicodemus. Every sales course I've ever heard of dictates that the seller *immediately* get on the good side of the prospective buyer. Salesmen are told to use flattery, to choose something positive about the prospect to comment on. They're instructed to show friendliness and openness. Above all, they have to keep smiling.

When many leaders get with the high and mighty of this world, they tend to water down their convictions—or at least carefully state everything in its most positive and acceptable form. They don't want to offend people, especially at the first meeting. Jesus didn't follow these rules.

Nicodemus, in the way he came to Jesus, implied that a man in his position would be ashamed to be seen publicly with this controversial new rabbi called Jesus. The Pharisee approached Jesus in a condescending manner, if not actually patronizing Him. In this way Nicodemus represents many in our society today who think they are conferring great honor on Christianity when they say, "We, the intellectual pundits of literature; we, the arbiters of taste; we, the guides of public opinion; we, the writers of newspapers, magazines, and periodicals; we, the television anchormen and commentators; we, the leaders of social and philanthropic movements—we recognize that Jesus was a great teacher."

But however patronizing and condescending Nicodemus may have been, his inadequate perception of Jesus didn't change one iota the Lord's "open-arms" policy. Neither should our society's condescension cause us to become aloof or bitter.

How did Jesus manage to confront Nicodemus courageously without becoming unloving? Let's look closely at the style of leadership He exhibited that night.

As a young rabbi from Nazareth who had no certificate from the authorities, Jesus was being presented with an unequaled opportunity for an opening into the very center of the Sanhedrin. There could be nothing half so sweet for an ardent young spiritual leader as early recognition by men of wisdom and influence that he too is a messenger from God. In his later years of ministry he might find the praise and acknowledgment cloying, but not at the beginning.

Jesus could have been sucked into flattery. He could have said, "I am honored that you came to see Me," or, "What a privilege it is for Me," or, "I am glad you recognized that I came from God." This would have made sense if the young rabbi were only seeking recognition.

By speaking out as He did, however, Jesus showed courage, even audacity—and compassion. He didn't try to be antiestablishment or to ridicule Nicodemus. Some leaders try to build their empires through putdowns, snickers, jibes, sarcasm, hidden anger, or ridicule; Jesus resorted to none of those devices.

The leadership style of Jesus is shown here to be as versatile as each situation calls for. When the crowds were gathered at the temple, Jesus did not hesitate to express His anger publicly at the money changers who had defiled God's house. But here He worked on the quiet side. After dark, in the stillness of the night, He did not hesitate to have a tough but patient intellectual debate with Nicodemus.

Not long ago I watched a televised discussion between a Christian leader and an avowed humanist. It saddened me that the Christian leader tried harder to gain the audience's acceptance than he did to boldly present the claims of Christ. The more heckling increased from the audience, the more watered-down the message of the Christian leader became.

Our secular society welcomes with open arms the element of the Christian church that willingly embraces all shades of belief. Our culture embraces churchmen who make no heavy moral demands. Our world is open to receive a spineless Christianity that sees God in everything and everything in God. But that is not the leadership style of Jesus.

Christ's leadership style calls for courage—for speaking the truth in love. There is a difference between love and compromise.

If we learn anything from the leadership style of Jesus, it is that truth comes before everything else. Jesus never "set people up" for His "sales pitch." He didn't soften them up with promises. At times He actually discouraged prospects from following Him, by pointing to the rigors and costs of discipleship. He wanted no one to embrace the faith without knowing what the future held for His followers.

The Cost of Courage

A friend worked for twenty years as a reservation agent for one of the world's largest airlines. During her last two years with that company, she got into trouble with her supervisors three times because of her honesty.

As the airline intermittently monitored incoming calls, it found that Barbara tried to give customers complete information about service and price. If the prospective customers needed to fly at a particular time and her airline did not have a flight scheduled she looked up information about *rival* airlines and gave out *that* information. Once she even told a customer to go on another airlines because the customer could save money on that flight!

Barbara felt she had to show integrity, though she wanted her company to make money. She might have lost her job.

THE LEADERSHIP STYLE OF JESUS

But she kept it until retirement—because the company received letters about her from customers. All of them thanked the airline for the refreshing honesty of this reservation agent. One letter went so far as to say, "I travel a lot, and I've never had anyone suggest another airline unless I insisted. She volunteered that information. I want you to know that from now on, you are my exclusive airline."

Until she retired, Barbara still got occasional negative feedback from her supervisor. But she said she would rather have negative marks in her personnel file than to be dishonest with people. Unfortunately, her company did not encourage other employees to follow Barbara's example—but they allowed Barbara to handle her job in the way she saw fit because it paid off.

Whether it seems to pay off or not, true leaders take their stands for what they believe in. One leader said it this way: "If I compromise on one principle with one person, where do I draw the line?"

The Courage of Christ

Nowhere did Jesus command His followers to show great courage. Nowhere did He say, "Never compromise on your values." He didn't need to! His example was enough.

In the second chapter of John, for example, our Lord stood against all the Jewish leaders of His day because they had made a place of worship into a trading house. He chased them out with whips and overturned their tables. He castigated them for their wicked practices.

Once when I taught that passage, a young and rising businessman in the class said, "I've always thought that was one of the dumbest things in the world. The next day they set those tables right back up and went about their business."

Before I could reply, a young housewife responded. "Sometimes we have to choose symbolic action," she said. "Jesus couldn't clean out the temple every day. He didn't intend to do that. He could have spent His entire ministry finding ways to overthrow tables and chase out moneymakers. He used that action as a platform for the whole Jewish nation; by one significant act, He showed them what He believed in and what He stood for."

I couldn't have come up with a better answer.

We do not need more moralists in today's society; the world is full of them. What we need are leaders who will courageously give direction. We need leaders who know and will tell the truth. We need not to be told of our duties; we need the Christlike courage to do what we already know we should do.

Courage in Battle

One leader said, "Leaders choose their battles. They can't win every one. They may even lose a few along the way. But they can win the war."

Leadership is often a battle, and the fight requires courage. Having courage doesn't mean you'll never fear or tremble; it doesn't mean you'll have no inner turmoil or never ask, "God, am I doing the right thing?" Having courage means you'll do what's *right*, regardless of the consequences.

Martin Luther, fiery reformer of the sixteenth century, was a true man of courage. He defied the church of his day, the Pope, and other religious and secular leaders. In 1521 he appeared before the German Diet in the city of Worms; though promised safe escort, he knew he risked his life by going. The same promise had been given to John Hus a century earlier, and they had burned him at the stake. Church leaders had promised Luther forgiveness if he would repent of his "errors" and return to the "true faith." Luther knew this promise also had little value since they considered promises to heretics nonbinding. He also knew the history of the two previous centuries, when thousands of Christians underwent torture, sometimes death, during the infamous Spanish Inquisition.

Luther arrived safely, but the court allowed him no opportunity to defend his beliefs. Instead he was presented with a list of his "errors." Knowing that the court could decide whether he lived or died, Luther nevertheless said the following when asked if he would recant:

> Unless I am convicted of error by the testimony of Scripture (since I put no trust in the unsupported authority of Pope or of councils, since it is plain that they have often erred and often contradicted themselves), by manifest reasoning I stand convicted by the Scriptures to which I have appealed, I cannot and will not recant anything, for to act against our conscience is neither safe for us, nor open to us. On this I take my stand. I can do no other. God help me. Amen (T.M. Lindsay, *A History of the Reformation,* Charles Scribner's Sons, p. 257).

Through the centuries God's leaders have made their stands. They have stood for truth, integrity, and righteousness, no matter what their field of labor.

Courage Goes to Work

Several years ago a Christian leader in Australia—let's call him Jim—worked for the government. During his first week of employment, his superior asked Jim whether he wanted "to get some overtime." Needing the money, Jim said yes.

The first evening he was to work overtime, Jim watched

as his fellow employees gathered around a table and began to play cards. When Jim asked for work, his supervisor said, "What work? Overtime means staying back and signing our names later than normal."

Jim was not intimidated by his superiors. Instead he rebuked them: "If we are paid to work, then we must work." Not only did the other employees resent Jim; they began to persecute him.

First they wouldn't allow him to work overtime anymore. Then the boss gave him all the hard jobs to tackle. Around the office Jim became known as a "Bible basher" (an Australian derogatory term for Christians). "Jesus freak" and "fanatic" were also added to the list of nicknames.

Jim stood his ground. His boss told him, "You're a nice guy—just forget about your fanaticism. Follow the crowd and you will make a lot more money."

"I must work if I am paid," Jim replied. "Playing cards during working hours when we are paid time-and-a-half is not what my Christian convictions are all about."

Finally things became impossible for Jim, and he had to leave. Before he left, the head of the department called him into his office and said that Jim's stand had changed the attitudes of other workers. People were talking about being conscientious at the highest level of that agency.

Jim's courage had made him a leader. His refusal to compromise with the status quo was honored by God, who has since blessed him bountifully both financially and spiritually. God has promised that *He will honor those who honor Him* (1 Sam. 2:30).

The Price of Courage
Christians who are leaders know that taking a stand can lead to financial loss, even unemployment. Employers may

accuse them of being disloyal. But courageous leaders know that pleasing God must come first in their lives.

The Apostle Paul struggled with the matter of pleasing God or winning the approval of others. The Book of Galatians brings this out strongly. Paul had taught the Galatians the Gospel message that God saves through faith in Christ— and nothing more. After Paul left the region of Galatia, a group of teachers turned up and told the church members that they had to believe in Jesus and practice circumcision.

Paul countered, "Absolutely not!" He knew that those men were teaching "a different gospel" (Gal. 1:6). He pleaded with the people not to listen to the Judaizers and finally said, "For do I now persuade men, or God? Or do I seek to please men? For if I still pleased men, I would not be a servant of Christ" (Gal. 1:10).

Those words took courage. They caused controversy; they angered people. Paul probably lost a lot of friends over the debate. But he took his stance because of principle. We can rejoice over that today, because Paul made it clear once and for all that being a Christian is based on *faith* in Jesus Christ. We do not "complete" our faith by practicing parts of Judaism or by requiring "Jesus and. . ."

Note the risk of this courageous leadership. The prevailing wisdom would have told Paul, "This approach could backfire. The Judaizers will be so angry that they will turn against Jesus. You must speak to them kindly." But Paul, like Jesus, didn't live by the prevailing wisdom. His leadership style was a cut above.

Nicodemus: the Rest of the Story
What about Jesus' encounter with Nicodemus, mentioned earlier? It was courageous, but in the final analysis was it effective?

A look at John's Gospel shows that Nicodemus later made a weak attempt to defend Jesus by asking the religious leaders not to condemn Him without a court trial: "Nicodemus (he who came to Jesus by night, being one of them) said to them, 'Does our law judge a man before it hears him and knows what he is doing?' They answered and said to him, 'Are you also from Galilee? Search and look, for no prophet has arisen out of Galilee'" (John 7:50-52).

Still later, however, Nicodemus took a real stance of courage. After Jesus' crucifixion, wealthy Joseph of Arimathea asked Pilate for permission to bury the Lord in his own tomb. Then comes Scripture's final mention of Nicodemus:

"And, Nicodemus, who at first came to Jesus by night, also came, bringing a mixture of myrrh and aloes, about a hundred pounds" (John 19:39). Together the two men placed Jesus' body in the tomb. By that act, Nicodemus openly declared his discipleship.

It had taken considerable time for Nicodemus to acknowledge that he was Christ's follower. But when the Cross came and it became more dangerous to avow discipleship, he found courage—or rather the courageous leadership of Jesus had infected him. Boldness seemed to flow into Nicodemus from that cross; he helped prepare and entomb the body of Christ.

No doubt when Nicodemus looked at Jesus on the cross he remembered that night in Jerusalem when the Lord had said, "Even so must the Son of man be lifted up" (John 3:14). Perhaps that memory forever ended all hesitation and doubt in Nicodemus' mind.

It had all begun when Jesus displayed courageous leadership in dealing with Nicodemus. That too is part of His leadership style.

PRINCIPLE 4:
IN CHRIST'S SERVICE,
I CAN HAVE COURAGE FOR EVERY
LEADERSHIP BATTLE.

CHAPTER FIVE

GENTLENESS

I've always admired the way Jesus spoke up to people. Today we would call Him assertive, because He usually let people know how He felt without putting them down. He didn't fold when His adversaries tried to push Him into a corner either. In John 8, for example, the Jewish leaders accused Jesus of being demon-possessed. He said, "I do not have a demon; but I honor My Father, and you dishonor Me (8:49).

Jesus also rebuked His disciples when they needed it. On His last night with the Twelve, He took water and a towel and started to wash each disciple's feet. Peter refused. "You shall never wash my feet!" (John 13:8)

Jesus answered firmly, "If I do not wash your feet. . .you will no longer be My disciple" (v. 9, GNB).

The Gentle Side
At other times, however, Jesus showed the gentle side of His nature Nowhere does this come out more clearly than in

the story of the woman caught in adultery. Jesus did not excuse her sin, but He did forgive. After her accusers left, Jesus said, "Neither do I condemn you; go and sin no more" (John 8:11).

In considering the leadership style of Jesus, we may be tempted to put so much emphasis on His initiative, moving ahead, and vision that we neglect His gentleness. This is another important element of leadership that Jesus exemplified beautifully.

When our Lord encountered those who plotted against Him, He could stand up to them and hold His own. But when He met with the common people—the people with needs—His gentle qualities came to the fore.

In one of the most poignant passages in the New Testament, Jesus and His disciples were followed until they needed a chance to rest. They climbed into a boat and left shore to get away.

> Many people, however, saw them leave and knew at once who they were; so they went from all of the towns and ran ahead by land and got to the place ahead of Jesus and His disciples. When Jesus got out of the boat, He saw this large crowd, and His heart was filled with pity for them, because they were like sheep without a shepherd. So He began to teach them many things (Mark 6:33-34, GNB).

Meek Isn't Weak

In our culture we tend to think of *gentle, humble,* and *meek* as words denoting *weakness.* These qualities may, in fact, indicate greater character and self-control than the "strength" that enables some to verbally lash out or eloquently argue with opponents.

Translators of the New Testament have not always been consistent in rendering these words. In Greek, meekness is *praotes,* gentleness is *epieikes* and kindness is *chrestotes*—yet all three have similarities in meaning. In the *King James Version* translators sometimes rendered *chrestotes* as kindness, other times as gentleness (see Titus 3:4; 2 Cor. 6:6; Eph. 2:7; Col. 3:12; Gal. 5:22). Another version of 2 Corinthians 6:6 translates the word as *sweetness. Mellow* might be another rendition. The same word is used when Jesus calls His yoke "easy" (Matt. 11:30), meaning that it does not irk or irritate.

The Apostle Paul mentioned gentleness as one of the fruits of the Spirit. I used to wonder about that. So much of what I read about Paul made me think he was a feisty little man, quick to set people straight, always to the point, eloquent in arguments. How could he put so much emphasis on a quality that he did not have in his own life? I have since come to understand that people can be straightforward *and* gentle and meek.

Three-part Gentleness

Gentleness combines three qualities. The first part is consideration or kindness. The gentle leader considers the feelings of others. He would never intentionally hurt or belittle them.

The second part of gentleness is submission. In the biblical sense, it means submission to the will of God—as does the word *meek.* Moses, whom God called the meekest man on the face of the earth (Num. 12:3), did not hesitate to oppose wrong or stand up for truth. He submitted to God's will.

Jesus also displayed this quality, submitting to the will of His Father. He might have taken an easier way out, but willingly went to the cross and refused all human honor.

A third facet of gentleness is being teachable—not too

proud to learn, and correctable. A truly gentle person never stops learning and continues to be open to new understanding.

This trait typifies a professional writer I know who leads two groups for people who are learning to write. Group members must bring in written material each week and let the others critique it. The leader feels it's the most valuable way to learn.

He believes this so strongly, in fact, that he frequently brings in his own current material. While his students don't always know how to evaluate properly, he still learns from their comments. "No writer ever gets so good that he or she can never get help from others," he says. That's an aspect of gentleness at work, and it's an important one for leaders to possess.

Gentle Strength

Around 1970 a short-lived series called "Gentle Ben" appeared on American television. Ben was a bear—a large, *strong* bear. But he was also loving toward the family that adopted him. He could be outraged and display plenty of physical strength, but he could also show a tender nature. That bear is the most concrete image of gentleness I can think of.

Gentleness has hidden strength. Some mistakenly think that gentle leaders are weak leaders; but if they have true, biblical gentleness, they also possess an inner reserve of power.

Gentleness in Action: Jesus and the Woman

As previously mentioned, the gentle side of Jesus' leadership is perhaps most clearly drawn in the story of the woman taken in adultery (John 7:53-8:11). Interestingly, some translations have questioned this as an authentic passage or place it in different contexts. One scholar commented, "the tone of the story, whether actually Scripture or not, shows us a characteristic picture of Jesus." We can find a similar picture in the Luke 7:36-50 story of the woman who anointed Jesus' feet at the home of Simon the Pharisee.

In the account of the woman caught in adultery, it's easy to focus on Jesus' telling response to the Jewish leaders who tried to trap Him—and to miss His attitude toward the woman. How that woman must have cowered in the midst of all those men who encircled her! The fear, the pain, and the guilt must have been overwhelming. Yet Jesus treated her as a person, not an object.

As the religious leaders brought the woman to Jesus, they appeared to have no consideration for her as a human being. They had one purpose in mind: to trap Jesus Christ. He not only stopped them from executing her, but shamed them at the same time.

For me, the most important aspect of the story is the way it ends. Jesus did not lecture the woman about her immorality as many leaders might do today. He did not warn her of the harm she had inflicted on herself and her family. He did not scold her and ask, "Why did you allow yourself to sink to such a condition?"

Instead He did two things:

First, *He accepted her.* "Woman, where are those accusers of yours? Has no one condemned you?. . .Neither do I condemn you" (John 8:10-11). Thus Jesus let her know His awareness of her sin, but laid no greater burden on her.

I believe most of us have enough guilt to carry without others laying more on us. When we fail, we know it. We tend to hate ourselves for being weak or think of ourselves as evil. We feel so much self-hatred we don't need anyone else to add to it.

Jesus spoke sharply to those who denied their sins and tried to hide their failures. But to those already overburdened with pain and a sense of failure, He was encouraging. He condemned sin, but gently lifted people up. That policy reminds me of something an old preacher friend said to me: "A sermon should do two things—comfort the disturbed and disturb the comfortable."

What was the second thing Jesus did for that woman? *He forgave her.* "Neither do I condemn you; go and sin no more" (v. 11).

I marvel at that statement; it's so simple and direct. Jesus said everything she needed to hear in those few words. He let her know she was forgiven, but warned her not to do it again. He didn't harp on her wrongdoing, lecture her about temptation, or confuse her with moralisms. He said, "Don't do it again." That's all she needed to hear. Today's errant followers need that kind of correction from gentle leaders.

Does Gentleness Work?

A friend of mine came from a poor family. The barest of necessities of life were provided him, but there was little else. Being bright and having an inquisitive mind, he loved to read. He went regularly to a pharmacy where they had a section of magazines; there he found he could hide in a corner and read the magazines, especially the comics. He treated them carefully so that no one would complain about torn pages.

One day he went beyond reading. He slipped a magazine inside his shirt before he left. A few days later he returned and, making sure no one saw him, he slipped in two. Before long he had set up a pattern of stealing the magazines.

Eventually the pharmacist caught him and made him pull

the magazines out of his shirt. Terrified, the boy wondered what the man would do. Would he call the police? Tell the boy's parents?

The pharmacist proceeded to talk to the boy quietly about taking property that did not belong to him. Then he did a surprising thing. He put his hand on the boy's shoulder and said, "Please, don't do that again."

Today my friend says, "I never did it again—and I never forgot that man. He could have been mean to me within his legal rights, but he treated me kindly."

It takes great strength to be gentle. Not every leader knows how to show the gentle side. Many of us make it harder by tending to look down on gentle people as weak, ineffective, perhaps even stupid. But Jesus said, "Neither do I condemn you; go and sin no more."

Gentleness may be a quality of leadership we have lost in many of our business dealings, our classrooms, our homes —even in our churches. We need to remember this aspect of the leadership style of Jesus:

PRINCIPLE 5:
ONLY THE TRULY STRONG LEADER
CAN BE TRULY GENTLE.

CHAPTER SIX

CUSTOM-BREAKING

One of the staff members in a local church reached the age of sixty-five. The personnel committee had established a policy years earlier that required mandatory retirement at that age. But the woman enjoyed good mental and physical health, and because of a government mixup on her social security she asked to go on working another year.

Still the personnel committee said, "We have a rule. We can't break the rule."

Some of us went to the head of the committee and asked, "Isn't she an excellent worker?"

"Oh, yes, she is. One of the best workers we've ever had."

"Isn't she filling a big gap?" we asked. "Isn't she holding down a responsible position?"

"Oh, yes, she is. She does the work of at least two people and does it quietly. She has the capacity to make things run smoothly around here."

"Then why are you forcing her out while she can still do her job well?" we asked.

"We really have no choice," the man answered. "Regulations, you know." He brought out the list of rules, opened it to the appropriate spot, and held it up for me to read. "There," he said. "See?"

"But who made the regulations?" I asked.

"We don't know. I mean, some personnel committee in the past. They were trying to look ahead, and laid down precise regulations for us to follow."

I discussed, argued, pleaded, urged, and begged, but the head of the personnel committee stood firm. No matter how much I argued or how emotional I became, he had one standard response: "The regulations say. . . ."

Jesus Encounters Regulations

As recorded in John 5:1-15, Jesus did a remarkable thing. A man with a crippling illness that had lasted thirty-eight years lay by a pool called Bethesda. Many other sick people also lay beside the pool because they believed that at certain times an angel came and stirred up the waters. After that occurred the first person in the water would receive healing.

Jesus came up to the disabled man and asked, "Do you want to be made well?" (v. 6) He did, and Jesus healed him.

After the man was healed, he took up his pallet and started to walk home. That might have been the ending of a wonderful little story. But Gospel-writer John added one detail—a detail that affected the way others would respond to the miracle. John wrote "And that day was the Sabbath" (v. 9).

As soon as the religious leaders heard about the healing, they didn't pause to rejoice. They didn't thank God for doing an amazing thing in their midst. They grew angry. They said to the man, "It is the Sabbath; it is not lawful for you to carry your bed" (v. 10).

CUSTOM-BREAKING

One might think these leaders would be happy that the man had been healed, delivered from thirty-eight years of misery. But because Jesus healed the man on the sacred Sabbath Day, when God had commanded people to do no work, they were enraged. They would have preferred that this man continue to be sick and hopeless for the rest of his life rather than receive God's mercy on their holy day.

Performing such a miracle gave more proof of the messiahship of Jesus. But His detractors didn't examine the evidence. They saw only His radicalism, His inability to fit their mold. Even in Jesus' day, religious institutions had become encrusted by rules and regulations that enslaved people, making them live to work instead of work to live. Rules, necessary as guidelines, had become chains. Regulations so bound these leaders that they made no consideration for human need.

Jesus broke their customs. In their eyes He had committed one of the worst possible sins. He had violated the Sabbath laws, and they could not overlook that. He tried to show them the difference between using rules and abusing them, between helping people and enslaving them, and used the occasion to tell His listeners of His special relationship with the Father.

This shows us another facet of the leadership style of Jesus. When He saw some good that needed to be done, he didn't ask, "What day is this?" The sick man needed healing. Jesus put compassion and mercy before laws.

Someone has said it this way: Jesus loved people and used things, but the religious leaders loved things and used people. This incident was not meant to encourage people to break the law habitually or to be antiestablishment; rather, Jesus was vividly illustrating that people must come before regulations.

Institutions and Regulations

During my graduate studies, I researched institutions and social movements. That's when I learned that at the founding of any institution—Christian or not—the founders criticize other, more established organizations. For instance, a new company that sells computer software will boast, *"We* can give *personal* service. The guys in the *big* company don't care about serving *their* customers."

When a new congregation or denomination is formed, the members often feel disenchanted with the established group from which they came. They perceive the older body as having become too rich, too impersonal, no longer caring for the people—and functioning only by rules and regulations. They may feel the established church is too concerned about keeping money coming into its coffers so that its programs will continue—not about feeding the sheep.

Then the *new* church or business grows large and becomes established. Eventually the new founders will hear the same accusations they made against their forerunners. And once again a radical, enthusiastic young leader, full of entrepreneurial spirit, will come forth and declare that "we" must do away with the silly rules that stop us from reaching out to people. "We" must be people-oriented.

Similarly, when God communicated the Law to Moses, He handed down regulations for the *good* of the community. Over the centuries leaders interpreted, reinterpreted, explained, and re-explained those basic regulations.

In time, deep-thinking teachers *added* to the laws through constant reinterpreting and explaining. Eventually every orthodox Jew had to observe 613 daily obligations. The same teachers divided the laws into those they called *weighty* (248 daily obligations) and those they called *light* (365 precepts). Breaking the light rules did not carry as great a penalty.

Back to Basics

Jesus' leadership style reversed that of the scribes, Pharisees, and priests. When they wanted to speak with authority, they said, "As Rabbi Hillel taught. . . ." They referred to a regulation, precept, or teaching by a famous predecessor.

Jesus, on the other hand, made statements like this one in the Sermon on the Mount: "You have heard that it was said. . . . But I say to you. . . ." (Matt. 5:27-44) He did not mean He wanted to contradict Moses' laws or destroy what God had commanded in the past. Rather He showed by such acts as the healing of the lame man that the religious leaders had made gods out of the commandments that were supposed to guide them to live in community and worship God.

In Jesus' day the leading scholars debated endlessly the question "What is the greatest commandment?"

Jesus clarified that easily enough when they asked Him—probably trying to trick Him—"Which is the first commandment of all?" (Mark 12:28)

Jesus answered by quoting from the Law of Moses: " 'You shall love the Lord your God with all your heart, with all your soul, with all your mind, and with all your strength. . . .' The second, like it, is this: 'You shall love your neighbor as yourself.' There is no other commandment greater than these" (vv. 30-31).

Jesus had a "back to basics" leadership style. He knew God's laws were meant to help, not hinder, people in living fulfilled lives. So He put the emphasis where it belonged—on compassion, love, faithfulness to others and to God—not on outward behavior.

Paul's Style

Paul displayed this Christlike leadership trait when he wrote to the churches in Galatia. A quicksand of rules had engulfed the believers there, threatening to overwhelm them. Paul tried to show how Christ had liberated them, and explained the concept of Christian liberty.

Doesn't this happen all the time in churches today? Many congregations seem spiritually dead because they rigidly hold to traditions begun hundreds of years ago. Though "respectable," they emphasize a *means* of worship that now blocks the *act* of worship.

Some overseas missionaries have also failed because they were too inflexible to exercise Christian liberty. Many built churches better suited for Boston or London than Africa or Asia, with Western architecture and pews, pulpits, choirs, and robes. They not only introduced elements totally alien to these cultures, but made them an integral part of worship.

I know missionaries, for example, who worked in East Africa during the 1930s and '40s. There they encountered people who had their own form of music, sung in a minor key with no regular meter. Well-meaning missionaries who began to teach them Western-style hymns translated into the local vernacular immediately ran into problems.

First, the missionaries insisted on regularity of the meter. "After all, that's the way music is supposed to be," one missionary said. They persisted in teaching the people Western music with its different tonal scale, sometimes giving up clarity if it interfered with the rhythm. Worse, the Westerners forbade the Africans to sing anything from African culture; the missionaries thought that represented heathenism. As far as I know, those Westerners didn't bother to listen to the indigenous songs and their meanings.

I wonder if Jesus might have said to those well-intentioned missionaries, "You care more about your musical tastes than you do about the needs of these people. But I say to you, let them rejoice, let them worship with their voices, their words, *and* their style of music."

How would some of those missionaries have responded? In the same way the rigid leaders did in Jesus' day, though less drastically. After Jesus healed the man by the pool, "For this reason the Jews persecuted Jesus, and sought to kill Him, because He had done these things on the Sabbath" (John 5:16).

Putting the First First

Jesus' style of leadership puts people first, regulations second. Human needs come first, traditions second. The kingdom of God comes first—and *everything* else second. In practical terms, that means leaders must sometimes violate "sacred" traditions and tear down barriers. Sometimes that takes great courage.

Leaders who follow the style of Jesus don't break traditions simply to break them. Customs can bring great benefits. Usually they come into being for good reasons. Yet when custom interferes with human need, leaders do well to consider breaking the rules.

This leads to our next principle:

PRINCIPLE 6:
TRUE LEADERS PLACE HUMAN NEEDS BEFORE HUMAN CUSTOMS.

The principle sounds fine. The difficulty comes in knowing how to apply it, because we are faced with so many traditions. Jesus could have used hundreds of examples to show how the religious leaders of His day had exploited and spiritually enslaved the people, but He selected one of the most important ones—the law of the Sabbath. Perhaps He cited this principle so that people could examine other customs, rituals, and regulations by the same criteria.

Sound custom-breaking goes back to Jesus' definition of the first commandment—loving God with all our hearts. He tied this to loving our neighbors as ourselves so tightly that it's practically the same commandment. How better can we show our love to God than by the way we treat people? The true leader uses love as the measure for breaking human customs to meet human needs.

CHAPTER SEVEN

GENEROSITY

A man entered college at age twenty-five. He had tried a lot of other things first, but finally realized he wanted to learn. During his second year, a rapport developed between him and one of his professors.

After a few months the professor said, "Bob, you have a mind like cotton; you absorb everything I teach. But even more, you have the kind of mind that won't settle for answers. You're asking your own questions."

A year later the same professor told Bob, "I've taught you everything I know. Frankly, you have ability beyond mine. I think you need to transfer to a different school where you'll find a fresh challenge." Despite his affection for Bob, the professor wanted his student to surpass him. Not many people act that generously.

A pharmacist saw promise in a young man who was a member of his church. He knew the young man had a lot of ability and wanted to go to college, but could not. The young man's parents had died and he, being the oldest son, had to work to support two younger brothers.

After much prayer for guidance, the pharmacist gave the two younger boys part-time work so that their older brother would not need to support them. Then he loaned the young man all the money he needed to get through school.

Five years later the young man had a master's degree and a secure future. Ready to start paying back, he came to his benefactor. "I figure I can pay you at the rate of $200 a month," he began.

The pharmacist shook his head. "I lent you that money, but I don't want it back. I want you to watch for a young person as deserving as you were and do the same thing for him or her."

That professor and that pharmacist had a spirit of generosity. That quality is necessary if one is to be a Christlike leader.

Jesus' Generosity

One event that illustrates the self-giving generous attitude of Jesus Christ is His feeding of the 5,000 (John 6:1-14). It is the only miracle recorded in all four Gospels, which indicates that it made a deep impression on those in the early church.

Jesus took one boy's lunch and multiplied the food so that He had enough to feed all the people present. The writers speak of 5,000 *men,* which means that this figure probably did not include the women and children present.

This miracle shows the generosity of Jesus in providing for people's needs. He could have sent the crowds home. He could have warned them in the morning of the long day ahead, and of their need for food. He could have shrugged it off as "not My problem."

The disciples, being realists, recognized that the people

must be hungry and were concerned about them. But from the disciples' standpoint Jesus owed the crowd nothing; He had not urged them to follow. So the disciples made a sensible suggestion: Send the people home before it gets too dark.

Who would have faulted Jesus for doing that? It would have made perfect sense to everyone. But Jesus didn't send them away; He provided for them. That's the generosity of Jesus Christ. He gives when we have no claims, no reason to ask, no expectations.

Jesus provided for people what they could not provide for themselves. In this case it was food. To the blind man in John 9, He gave sight. At the wedding feast in John 2, the guests had no reason to expect Jesus to provide wine. But Jesus, in an act of generosity, provided for them. This brings us to the next leadership principle:

PRINCIPLE 7:
TRUE LEADERS GIVE GENEROUSLY.

Executive Generosity
Contrary to popular myth, good leaders do not make it to the top by stepping all over people. We sometimes think of those "at the top" as having an "I made my own way; you make yours" attitude. But my experience has been the opposite. Those who reach the top—especially those who have had to come from the bottom—know the hardships and disappointments of the corporate climb, and the importance of getting help.

A few years ago a national magazine surveyed the chief

executive officers of twenty of the nation's top corporations. Each said he had gotten the biggest boost when someone higher up saw him, became impressed with his ability, and befriended him. One leader remarked, "Every time [my mentor] moved up, he took me one notch up with him."

When I read the article, one listed quality surprised me: generosity. Those who make it to the top, it seems, do not represent the kind of people who trample on those who are no longer of use to them. These leaders work well with others, and that's how they got to the executive suite. They helped others, sometimes when help could have resulted in competition for themselves.

Since reading that article I've met several Christian executives or know of them through others. Not all of them exemplify generosity, but many do.

When I say generosity, I mean self-giving with no expectation of return. I don't mean giving to get. I don't mean helping someone and reminding him, "You owe me one."

Generous leaders don't stop at being mentors either. They give a helping hand to a wider circle of people. They encourage. They want others to succeed.

The late Cecil B. Day, Sr. was such a leader. He founded Day's Inns of America, a chain whose motels now number well over 300. The motels were designed and priced to help lower-income travelers as well as government employees and other per-diem workers.

Cecil came from a modest background to found the multi-million-dollar chain. He was known as a man who worked hard in order to give money to causes that honored God.

Before his death, Cecil gave away all of his part of the estate. He had always given a chance to deserving young people, evangelists, ministers, and other Christian workers. His life was a life of giving.

How Leaders Give

Generosity doesn't only mean giving money. Leaders who understand the concept of Jesus' love know that they can give of *themselves*—often in ways that surpass giving material things.

How do they do it?

1. *They give their time.* Leaders, rather than hoarding time, use it to serve in many ways. Some of the church's most effective laypeople come from leadership positions in business. One regional sales manager for a meat-packing company said, "I give my employer my best. At the church, I use the principles I know from business to serve Jesus Christ." This busy manager heads the evangelism program at his church.

2. *They give their attention.* When one highly paid executive took his present position, he told his staff, "My door is open. If you need someone to talk to, I'll try to be available to listen."

Sixteen years later he has not changed his policy. Employees can't always get in as soon as they wish, but somehow he manages to make room for them. One secretary at his company says, "A problem came up at home that nearly devastated me. I called him because I needed to talk to someone. I know his busy schedule so I asked him, 'Are you too busy to talk to me a few minutes? I know how busy. . . .' "

"I'm never too busy for people," that executive answered. He stayed on the line with her for twenty minutes.

"He didn't solve my problem," the secretary recalls, "but he made me know he cared. Just his taking time to listen helped take away a lot of the pressure and the pain."

3. *They give of their experience.* The best leaders have learned many lessons in climbing toward the top. When asked, they're willing to pass on what they have learned.

One top management man said to his junior staff of eight, "I've got four more years before I plan to retire. I'll help you out in any way I can, but I won't give unsolicited help. You ask for it and you'll get it."

He didn't say it, but he intended that one of his staff would succeed him when he retired at age 58. One *did* succeed him. She was a highly motivated grandmother of forty-three who took his offer at face value. She watched him in operation, asked questions, and kept looking for more efficient ways to do things. He generously gave the help he'd promised.

The Giving Principle

Jesus said, "Freely you have received, freely give" (Matt. 10:8). Paul quotes Jesus as saying, "It is more blessed to give than to receive" (Acts 20:35).

The principle here is that we never lose by giving. We can only gain. To cynics that may sound strange, but it works. As leaders give of themselves, they produce better staffs, better relationships. Giving makes the Golden Rule a practical way of life.

By nature, however, most of us would prefer not to give. We usually learn generosity because someone has shown us by example. We have been helped by a benefactor, a friend, coworker, or boss and want to do likewise for another.

A Generous Spirit

Generosity comes in all forms. When leaders plan ahead for those who will follow, making the road a little easier, that's generosity. When leaders equip, teach, exhort, and encourage workers to stretch themselves, that's generosity; they don't have to do that for workers and might even have less problems if the workers stayed in their current positions.

But whatever form it takes, real generosity comes from deep within. It is not expressed to gain appreciation or loyalty from others.

One of the most generous-spirited men of God I've ever met is a man of limited education. He doesn't even have a lot of outstanding talents. I'll call him Claude.

While holding down a full-time job of hard manual labor, Claude became concerned for people in a poor section of his city. With his wife and two daughters, he started a small church in a rented house. People slowly started to come to church. Six years passed before the fellowship grew enough that Claude could quit his job and work full time at the church.

Eventually a young man who had met Jesus Christ in Claude's church left the congregation. One Sunday, while I visited Claude in his home, that young man called on the phone.

After talking for a while, Claude came back to the table and told his wife and daughters who had called. "He wants to start a church down the street," Claude said of the young man. The two of them would be trying to reach the same neighborhood.

"What did you tell him?" Claude's wife asked.

"Why, I said, 'Come on. There's plenty of people for both of us.'" As he smiled Claude's sincerity showed plainly. His last words to the young man had been, "You start at one end of the street, and I'll start at the other—and we'll meet in the middle."

That's generosity!

By contrast, a suburban pastor in another city had built a good-sized church. He became concerned about reaching those in a new housing developing even farther out of the city. Being part of a denomination that plans churches in concert with existing ones, he and members of the congregation informed three other churches of their idea: "We plan to open a satellite church and keep it going until it's big enough to stand on its own."

Representatives of one church, five miles from the new congregation's projected location, howled. "You can't go in there!" they cried. "That's drawing from our target area!"

The vision-minded church backed down, assuming the protesting congregation would work hard at reaching the members of the new community. Five years later, however, they still had done nothing. It seemed they didn't want to go in, but didn't want others to go in either! Unfortunately, we find that attitude often in our world—even among God's people.

But generous leaders have no such mindset. They find joy and pleasure in giving and sharing. They understand the principle that true leaders, like Jesus, give generously.

CHAPTER EIGHT

TRUTHFULNESS

The TV drama led up to a dramatic moment. The doctor had examined the husband and run a dozen tests. Now the doctor was approaching the wife with the results.

"Tell me, doctor," she said.

"Do you want the truth?" he asked.

"Yes, of course."

I've watched that scene on TV a dozen times, and I've even heard it happen in real life. I always wonder, *What else could the person answer?* How many would openly say, "No, please lie to me. Make me feel good"?

I suspect that many of us don't want to know the truth about a lot of things. We find ways of hiding from it or covering it up. I've seen it happen in sharing groups, growth groups, and prayer groups. It starts when one person confronts another. The other person immediately starts wiggling away or denying what the confronter has said.

No one likes his or her less-than-perfect actions exposed. We're just as bad about hearing compliments; we hurriedly negate them. We simply do not know how to handle truth.

What Is Truth?

An old joke goes, "There are three sides to every story: your side, the other person's side, and the truth." The humor of that statement should strike home with us. We tend to slant facts in our favor—by omission of data or adding to the truth.

The Gospel of John recounts an amazing dialogue between Jesus and Pilate on the subject of truth. It occurred when the Jewish leaders brought the Lord to the governor for judging and sentencing. When asked whether He was a king, Jesus said, "You say rightly that I am a king. For this cause I was born, and for this cause I have come into the world, that I should bear witness to the truth. Everyone who is of the truth hears My voice." (John 18:37).

Pilate followed up with another question: "What is truth?" (v. 38) He must have expected no answer, because immediately he turned to the Jewish leaders and said, "I find no fault in Him." Pilate must have assumed no one could answer the question, "What is truth?"

But Jesus had already answered Pilate's question at another time recorded in the Gospel of John. On the evening of His pre-arrest farewell to His disciples, He declared that He was "the way, the truth, and the life" (14:6).

Jesus embodies truth, stands for truth, and refuses to deviate from it. No one could provide a better example of truthfulness for us to follow than He does. As the prologue to the fourth Gospel says, "The Law was given through Moses, but grace and truth came through Jesus Christ" (1:17). The writer doesn't mean that no truth existed before Jesus came to earth—only that Christ *is* the ultimate truth.

As disciples of the truth, we have a responsibility to be truth-tellers. While none of us sees or knows *all* truth, we have no excuse for avoiding it. If we call ourselves Christians, we imply among other things that we stand for what is true. Notice how Paul put truth at the start of this well-known list:

> Finally, brethren, whatever things are true, whatever things are noble, whatever things are just, whatever things are pure, whatever things are lovely, whatever things are of good report, if there is any virtue and if there is anything praise-worthy—meditate on these things (Phil. 4:8).

In leadership, perhaps more than anywhere else, truth must be allowed to stand. If people can't trust the word of their leaders, whom can they trust? If leaders lie or handle the truth carelessly, what kind of example do they set for those they lead?

Speaking the Truth

We can't merely talk *about* truth; we must also learn to speak the truth itself. That's not always easy to do.

Years ago, for instance, several of us listened to a well-known speaker at a convention. None of us had heard him before, though he had acquired the reputation of being outstanding. None of us liked his message very much that night; he produced a collage of five messages and tried unsuccessfully to blend them.

Because he was a close friend of a couple I knew well, I had phoned earlier that day and invited him to have coffee with us afterward. He had accepted. Now, after introductions around the table, he asked, "How did you like my message?"

He had thrown quite a bombshell! I watched the faces of the others as they struggled with how to answer. The first, being diplomatic, said, "You spoke with energy and sincerity. You really like doing public speaking, I could tell. I am sure you touched many people."

The second, a little less intimidated, said, "You tried hard, didn't you? Bet you put a lot of preparation into that message."

That brought a smile to the speaker's face. Then he turned to me.

I didn't know what to say. I hadn't liked the message particularly; he had rambled a lot and misapplied Scripture a little. I didn't want to lie, and I couldn't think as quickly as the second fellow. To say nothing would be tantamount to saying, "I didn't like it," and I didn't want to hurt his feelings.

Finally I said, "I'd better pass on that one. I just wasn't with it today. I couldn't keep my mind focused, so you'd better not ask me."

My answer didn't please me. I wished I could have lovingly said something like, "I did not like your message. If you're interested, perhaps we could get together later and I'll go into detail."

I talked about my dilemma later with a friend, who said, "If people don't want to hear the truth, they shouldn't ask for it." I didn't respond to my friend either. But I suspect that speaker had wanted positive feedback, perhaps flattery— not the truth.

Being truthful is a problem for me, one I face often. Bald-faced lies seldom escape my lips; I'm more troubled by half-truths, innuendos, silences. I smile when I'm mentally resisting. I avoid confrontation because I don't want to hurt another person. Too often I end up not speaking the truth— at least not the whole truth.

Mishandling Truth

When we speak less than truth, we lie. There are many ways to do that. Here are a few:

- Singing hymns of dedication like "Have Thine Own

Way, Lord," or "Take My Life, and Let It Be" but holding back on our commitment.
- Staying silent when we should speak up. Our silences often imply agreement or consent.
- Making promises we have no intention of fulfilling.
- Saying to people, "You must come and visit me," knowing we would feel put upon if they did.
- Allowing others to believe we have made spiritual achievements which we haven't.

Unfortunately, our world excuses lies—and sometimes even encourages them. One personnel expert told a meeting of executives that American business has gotten so used to lies on job applications that employers sometimes see truthful applicants as fools not worth hiring. Truth-tellers are supposedly not "sharp" enough to succeed.

Is it any wonder that some leaders don't want to appear naive by telling "nothing but the truth"?

The Oath

Our struggle with speaking less than the full truth should surprise no one. As the Bible indicates, we are habitually dishonest. Genesis 3 shows how our first parents strayed from the truth when God confronted them with their disobedience.

Perhaps that is the biggest reason for requiring an oath in legal matters. Doing so recognizes our natural tendency not to tell the truth.

The Jews of old are said to have had a saying: "One who gives his word and changes it is as evil as an idol-worshiper." Thus lying was a serious matter since no sin was considered more repugnant than idolatry. Taking an oath in those days invoked God as a witness that the speaker uttered only the truth. That was surely part of the intent of the commandment, "You shall not take the name of the Lord your God in vain" (Ex. 20:7).

That commandment condemns making promises in the name of God that cannot or will not be fulfilled. In Numbers 30:2 God declares, "If a man vows a vow to the Lord, or swears an oath to bind himself by some agreement, he shall not break his word; he shall do according to all that proceeds out of his mouth."

Originally the oath referred only to serious matters, such as those dealing with life and death. As time went on, people started using the oath frivolously.

Among Arabs of today in the Middle East, I have heard oaths sworn for the most meaningless purposes. Once while I bargained with a tradesman for a curio of less than two dollars' value, he declared, "This is my final price. On the honor of God, I can go no lower. Already I make no profit on this sale. I swear by my God."

We both knew he was lying. Eventually he came down a few more cents on his "final" price. His oath meant nothing.

In contrast, Jesus said in the Sermon on the Mount, "Do not swear at all. . . .But let your 'Yes' be 'Yes' and your 'No,' 'No.' For whatever is more than these is from the evil one" (Matt. 5:34, 37).

Jesus and Truth

Jesus not only taught that we should tell the truth; He embodied truth itself. After His betrayal, our Lord stood before the high priest who asked Him questions.

> Jesus answered him, "I spoke openly to the world. I always taught in synagogues and in the temple, where the Jews always meet, and in secret I have said nothing. Why do you ask Me? Ask those who heard Me what I said to them. Indeed they know what I said (John 18:20-21).

Jesus never denied the truth, but He didn't flaunt it either. He usually allowed people to perceive truth for themselves. He did not flatly tell His disciples that He was the Christ; for example; they eventually grasped who He was. That's how Jesus lived out the truth.

Interestingly, no matter what the list of accusations against Jesus, the charge of lying was not included. His enemies said He blasphemed by counting Himself an equal with God; they called Him a man possessed with demons; they charged Him with working on the sacred rest day because He healed the sick then. But even His worst detractors could not catch Him in a lie—because He told the truth.

Truth and Love

It's not enough just to speak the truth. *How* we speak it matters too.

Don't we all know people who speak the truth—bluntly? One man I know expresses his opinions on anything, regardless of how it sounds. He then defends his actions: "People know where I stand, and I don't believe in beating around the bush." No one ever accuses him of hypocrisy or deceit, but they do consider his words devoid of love, compassion, or kindness.

Christians need to speak the truth. But Paul says, "Speaking the truth in love, [we] may grow up in all things into Him who is the Head—Christ" (Eph. 4:15).

When we speak truth indifferently and it hurts others, we're wrong. When we speak out to belittle or degrade, the Holy Spirit is not speaking through us. Sometimes truth itself *does* hurt, and we can't always prevent that; but we can check our motivations for speaking.

Someone once said to me, "The Holy Spirit is a gentleman. A gentleman never behaves rudely or unkindly." God clothes truth in kindness. That leads to our next principle:

PRINCIPLE 8:
REAL LEADERS SPEAK THE TRUTH IN LOVE.

For some leaders, perhaps, lying holds no temptation. For most of us, however, it is all too easy to misuse truth. We need to follow the example of Jesus Christ in this area.

He spoke the truth even when popularity required a lie. He spoke the truth even when it meant crowds would desert Him (John 6:66). He spoke the truth because He *is* the truth and cannot deny Himself.

For many the struggle for truthfulness may be a lifelong battle. That only means we must be on guard and work at it. But we have the example of the way, the truth, and the life before us always. And we can continue to remind ourselves that true leaders love truth—and so does God.

CHAPTER NINE

FORGIVENESS

On November 14, 1940 the German Luftwaffe bombed the city of Coventry, England. It became the longest air raid over Britain during Word War II. When the bombing ended, residents surveyed the results and saw that their beautiful cathedral had been razed.

But at least some of the residents did not allow the tragic, pointless destruction of their place of worship to serve as an excuse for revenge. The next day members of that congregation took two irregular, charred beams from the roof, tied them together, and set them up at the east end of the ruins where the altar had been. The beams formed a cross. The parishioners printed two words on a sign and placed it at the foot of the cross: "Father Forgive."

In my home I keep a replica of that cross. The real one still stands next to the rebuilt cathedral. I hope it will stand there as long as human life exists to remind the world that even in the midst of devastation we can still cry out the words of Jesus, "Father, forgive them for they know not what they do" (Luke 23:34).

Jesus the Forgiver

The first believers learned forgiveness through the example of Jesus Himself. In the darkest moment of His life, He pleaded with the Father to forgive His executioners. A year or so later, the first known Christian martyr, Stephen, did the same. As the heavy stones struck Him, taking away his life, he prayed, "Lord, do not charge them with this sin" (Acts 7:60).

Forgiveness not only says, "I hold nothing against you." It wants the guilty person or people forgiven by God as well. We sometimes find it hard to ask that and really mean it. But as Jesus and Stephen showed, it can be done.

Jesus also taught forgiveness when He showed His disciples how to pray (Luke 11:1-4). When people in some churches recite the Lord's Prayer week after week, they may be unaware of what they're saying. But if we all took those words seriously, how many of us would feel like saying the prayer at all? When we pray, "Forgive us our debts (or trespasses)," we then say, "as we forgive. . . .The obvious meaning is that we ask God to forgive us in the same way we forgive others. Do we really want that to happen?

Why and How to Forgive

Over the years since my conversion to Jesus Christ, I've thought a great deal about forgiving. I've seen that God commands us to forgive both in the Old and New Testaments, and I've believed God never commands us to do anything we cannot do.

One day I understood the meaning of that phrase, "as we forgive." It has to do with our understanding of forgiveness. I saw that we can forgive others *only when we understand what it means to be forgiven ourselves.*

It's like the commandment to love our neighbors as we

love ourselves. Psychologists have reminded us that we cannot love other people until we know what it means to *be* loved. If I had never felt my parents or others loved me, for example, the behavioral scientists tell me I would have no true concept of love—especially the self-giving aspects of it. I would have to *experience* it before I could *express* it.

Those of us who have received Christ as Saviour *have* experienced forgiveness. Thus we can forgive others. To understand how to forgive, we need to study God's example.

In John 3:16-17 we find the why and how of God's forgiveness:

> For God so loved the world that He gave His only begotten Son, that whoever believes in Him should not perish but have everlasting life. For God did not send His Son into the world to condemn the world, but that the world through Him might be saved.

Because God loves the creatures He created, He provided for their salvation through Jesus Christ. God's love is the why of forgiveness; His Son is the how.

In John 8:1-11 the story of the woman taken in adultery shows God's forgiveness in action. Jesus told her, "Go and sin no more."

That story uplifts but in a way can also discourage. Think again of Jesus' instruction to the woman—not to sin again. He meant just that—*never again.*

I would like to believe that the woman never committed adultery again. But what about other sins? Did she lose her temper, commit a selfish act, tell a lie, covet? Of course she did! Then what? Would Jesus have forgiven her *again?*

In 1 John 2:1, the first part of the answer sounds much like the words of Jesus: "My little children, these things I write to you, that you may not sin." That expresses God's will for His people at all times: *Don't sin.* But the rest of 1 John 2:1

shows us the concept of grace: "And if anyone sins, we have an Advocate with the Father, Jesus Christ the righteous." That's the principle of forgiveness. God opposes sin: yet knowing our fallen nature, He makes a way for us to be reconciled to Him.

So does the Christian leader. He opposes wrongdoing among his followers or detractors, but is able to forgive and mend the relationship.

Forgiving and Forgetting

Forgiving means erasing a wrong. In my own experience, I realize that I have truly forgiven when my pain over the wrong has decreased and I feel no turmoil over the situation; I can talk about the incident and not feel my stomach tighten or my voice become constricted.

Once the pain goes away, the memory slowly fades—particularly the part about the wrong done to me. One day, for example, I told about a man I'd known ten years earlier. The man had hurt me deeply through something he said or did, but strangely enough I could not remember what had happened. For a few seconds I tried to recall what caused the problem but couldn't. Then it struck me: I didn't *need* to remember because I had forgiven him. I silently gave thanks to God for my inability to remember the problem. I was glad to remember the important part—the resolution.

Some people, when asked to forgive, say "I'll forgive you, but I'll never forget." I wonder what they think they're achieving by not forgetting. To remember means to keep the problem burning inside; forgetting means putting the fire out.

Eunice, a former missionary to Liberia, told a story about forgiveness that has long remained with me. An African man worked for her, and one day she caught him stealing clothes from her house.

"Please forgive me," he pleaded. "I did wrong. I promise not to do it again."

She forgave him and allowed him to continue working for her. But less than a month passed before she caught him stealing again. "Look at you!" she said. "You've stolen again!"

The bright fellow stared at her and yelled back, "What kind of Christian are you?"

Eunice, dumbfounded, had no idea how to respond. "If you forgave me, you do not remember it," the man said. "If you do not remember it, such a thing did not happen."

Aside from the fact that he used questionable logic to talk his way out of his wrongdoing, the story struck home with me. I've known of people who say they forgive another— then wait until the person makes another mistake. "Aha!" they say. "Just as I thought!"

A Mark of Leadership

One true mark of the Christian leader is his or her ability to forgive. When people fail us, especially when we perceive it as deliberate, we can do no better than to remember the words of Jesus: "Neither do I condemn you. Go and sin no more."

But true forgiveness takes divine help. Most of us prefer revenge—or at least being proven right before we forgive.

Haven't we all had our feelings hurt by church members, coworkers, or employees who said unkind things about us— sometimes even untrue things? We all have at least one relative who rankles us every time we meet, managing to offend us in some fashion. How can we handle those situations?

We can dwell on what the offender has done to us. We can

keep reminding ourselves of his failures, his evil intentions, his meanness. Or we may cry out for "justice" when we really mean "Prove me right," or "Make the miserable dog more miserable until she repents."

We may try to "get even." I once heard a sermon on how to get even with your enemies. The pastor said something like this:

> Most of us want to get even, and we can. Jesus told us how. He said, "You have heard that it was said, 'You shall love your neighbor and hate your enemy.' But I say to you, love your enemies, bless those who curse you" (Matt. 5:44).
>
> You want to get even? Pray for the obnoxious, the thoughtless, the insensitive, the hardhearted, the rude, and the mean.

The pastor ended his sermon by admonishing, "Be careful about your prayers. They not only change other people, but sometimes they backfire and change us! And that's really getting even!"

If anyone had reason to get even with enemies, it was Jesus. But when they brought Him to the high priest, the Lord didn't even try to explain or to prove His innocence. He said "I spoke openly to the world. I always taught in synagogues and in the temple, where the Jews always meet, and in secret I have said nothing" (John 18:20).

Later, standing before Pilate, Jesus had His second chance to defend Himself. Yet at no time did He try to show the outrageousness of the charges, the falseness of His accusers, or the sinfulness of their actions. In the entire encounter with Pilate He said nothing in His defense (John 18:28-38). This was not the typical action of an offended man; it was the style of Jesus, the forgiving One.

Steps to Reconciliation

Effective leaders are forgiving leaders. We can't work with people if we hold grudges against them, after all. Here are three things we can do to pave the way toward forgiving others:

1. *Self-examination.* Sometimes we have to ask ourselves why we hold grudges, why we end up hurt and angry. As a godly friend said to me, "No one can hurt your feelings but yourself. Other people only touch a tender part of your life that you have not yet surrendered to Jesus Christ."

Others may touch our sense of inferiority, our fear of looking foolish, our feeling of inadequacy about our jobs. Such people might actually be doing us a favor by pointing out areas we need to work on.

2. *Pray for Enemies.* Why not write down the names of your detractors, rivals, and critics and hold them up to God every day? Don't pray, "God, please convict John and bring him to his senses." Instead say, "Father, help me understand John. Make me compassionate toward him."

3. *Expect Healing.* We need to work for reconciliation. We can expect it to happen. We can approach each hurt with an openness that says, "God, I know I'm going to forgive and forget what John has done." It can happen—if we allow it to.

PRINCIPLE 9:
LEADERS CAN FORGIVE BECAUSE THEY HAVE BEEN FORGIVEN.

---

3 Part

THE TEMPTATIONS OF LEADERSHIP

CHAPTER TEN

POWER

Jesus did everything wrong, according to the rules of some leadership programs. His mistake was His constant integrity. He never played games nor deceived. No one could mistake His intentions who really wanted to know.

The religious leaders of His day never opened themselves to find out; however. Jesus posed a threat to them and their authority. They stood against Him from the beginning because they knew He threatened their power base.

When many people think of leadership, they think of power. We need to look at this matter of power, because it applies to leadership in the church, business, schools, homes—anywhere two or more human beings gather. We need to see how Jesus differed from other leaders in His concept and use of power.

Two Kinds of Power
When I talk about power, I'm thinking of the ability to influence or induce behavior. There are two kinds of

power, humanly speaking:

Position power refers to the influence leaders have because of their positions in the church, business, or family. While church members might not volunteer if just anybody asked, for example, they more likely will respond to the request of the pastor.

Personal power comes from the charisma, personality, or ability of a leader. During World War II, Prime Minister Sir Winston Churchill exercised great personal power in his ability to motivate England's citizens.

In May 1940, during Britain's darkest hours, Churchill made his first speech as Prime Minister in the House of Commons. He concluded with, "I have nothing to offer them but blood, sweat, toil, and tears." A seemingly defeated nation had its morale lifted and rallied behind him.

President Franklin Roosevelt pulled American through a great economic depression and guided the country during World War II. He is especially remembered for his declaration which became a rallying call during troubled times: "We have nothing to fear but fear itself." Through the strength of his own personality, he offered the people of his country confidence in the future.

There is danger in personal power, of course. It can become manipulative. Leaders can become tyrants, as in the case of Jim Jones.

That was part of the temptation faced by Jesus in the wilderness (Matt. 4:1-11). The devil took Him to the highest mountain and offered Him all the kingdoms of the world. That was an attempt to manipulate Him to thirst for power. Even turning stones to bread would have involved manipulating the forces of nature for personal gain. Jumping from the temple would certainly have been an attempt to manipulate God the Father to rescue His Son.

Power Plays

In the church today, power plays are mostly verbal. This has not always been the case. At times they have involved punishment such as excommunication (or shunning, which still goes on amoung certain sects), physical torture, even death.

Today leaders usually maintain power through the following means:

- persuasion/manipulation
- creating feelings of guilt, shame, or ignorance
- making threats
- belittling or biting humor
- making appeals

Let's examine these one by one.

Persuasion/Manipulation

The infamous Jim Jones of Jamestown, Guyana may have exemplified this style of power leadership better than any other modern figure. He persuaded converts with his charismatic personality, convincing them that he could and would make life better for them.

Once converts became part of his People's Church, Jones' persuasive methods often turned to a demonic form of manipulation. Legitimate persuasion uses logic, facts, reason; the warped kind hints that the subject is being uncooperative ("You don't want people to think you're not cooperating and giving your best to God, do you?") or unreasonable ("I knew you would understand if we talked about this. People know you as a reasonable person, and I've been telling them that you are not a troublemaker"). In the end Jones' manipulation killed him and most of his followers.

This perversion of persuasion prevents individuals from thinking and acting on their own. In John 7:45-52, Nicodemus tried to stand up for Jesus by asking if the law judged a man without a trial. The Pharisees shut him up by asking, "Are you also from Galilee? Search and look, for no prophet has arisen out of Galilee" (7:52). Poor Nicodemus had no chance; they ganged up on him. He would have appeared foolish to say anything more. This is a typical ploy of manipulative leaders.

Guilt, Shame, and Ignorance

I am convinced that in churches this form of power per-vades more than any other. We leaders, often solely by virture of our offices, have the ability to induce feelings of guilt, shame, and ignorance in many people. And we do it subtly.

For example, Anna has not attended the adult Sunday School class for three weeks in a row. Her teacher meets her on the street and says, "Anna, where have you been? I've missed you the past three Sundays." On the one hand the question shows genuine concern. But it also calls for an explanation; it makes a demand on Anna. When the teacher asks, "Where have you been?" Anna must offer an excuse as though she were a third-grade pupil who missed a day of school. Consciously or not, she is led to feel guilty.

Sometimes leaders try to portray those who disagree as ignorant. "If you knew all the facts, you would see things differently," the leader says. That implies ignorance as well as unreasonableness so that the follower is less likely to question further.

If a worker has failed in any way, small or large, the power-player may say, "You don't want to fail again, do you?" Some leaders make the point with more finesse, but their words still remind the follower of past mistakes—evoking shame and perhaps guilt.

Threats

In the commercial world, leaders' financial threats often force people to submit or leave. Fear of being fired, not getting pay raises, and receiving poor ratings on the annual job review are exploited to hold employees in line.

Sometimes the threat doesn't have to be one the leader can personally carry out. Others are made the "bad guys":

- "Well, if you want to look foolish, go ahead and push this idea."
- "While I have nothing against your idea, you know that the rest of the congregation (or board or committee) will shoot it down, don't you?"
- "I'll go with you to the committee, but if they laugh at us, don't blame me."
- "A lot of people have been considering proposing you as an elder, but if they begin to think of you as a troublemaker, they might reconsider."

Using threats is not a new misuse of leadership power. In John 9, after Jesus healed the blind man, the Pharisees pressured the man's parents to help them in their campaign against Christ:

They called the parents of him who had received his sight. And they asked them, saying, "Is this your son, who you say was born blind? How then does he now see?" His parents answered them and said, "We know that this is our son, and that he was blind; but by what means he now sees we do not know, or who opened his eyes we do not know. He is of age; ask him. He will speak for himself." His parents said these things because they feared the Jews, for the Jews had agreed already that if anyone confessed that He was Christ, he would be put out of the synagogue (John 9:- 18-22).

Belittling, Biting Humor

This may be the cruelest kind of power play. The leader who uses it ridicules the victim's suggestions so that they appear to have no value. The leader usually keeps a smile plastered on his face and his voice remains light and friendly; if challenged, he can always say any of the following:

- "Can't you take a little teasing? Why are you getting so upset?"
- "You have to be kidding!"
- "Ha ha! You have a real sense of humor, Tom. But I'm sure you don't actually mean that, so let's move on."

A friend of mine became aware of this power play when he worked one Christmas season with a hostel for international students. My friend smiled a lot and seemed to work well with the students. But one day two young Middle Eastern men said to him, "You smile much of the time, and that means you are happy and cooperative, does it not? You say we do not have to go on some of the trips you have arranged. And you still smile. But if we do not go, you also say words that make us know we have displeased you. All the while you continue to smile, even when you say things to us such as 'You're not too tired to go.' Please forgive us, but we do not understand."

My friend then realized his error. Unconsciously he had wanted everyone to attend each function, though he had told them differently. His words of biting humor, delivered with a smile, had confused the students. "It was a valuable lesson for me," he said later. "I never realized how I used that as a ploy to get my way with people."

Making Appeals

Sometimes leaders just plain beg. Their pleas may not sound like questions, but are nevertheless appeals to loyalty, sympathy, or hierarchy:

- "I am your pastor, you know. And I hope you don't think I would intentionally do anything wrong."
- "You understand that the council only *advises*, but I actually make the final decision."
- "You know, when you joined the church (or became a Sunday School teacher or were elected to the office of deacon), you promised to subject yourself to the authority and discipline of the church. As your friend and leader, I appeal to you. . . ."
- "I'm only trying to do my best around here. I had hoped I could count on your support. You're one of the spiritual-minded ones. I think highly of your opinion."

These quotes speak for themselves.

Jesus' Answer to Power

Perhaps the best place to see Jesus' use of power is John 13. The chapter records that after Jesus ate with His disciples, before His crucifixion, He washed their feet. In those days the lowest servant in a household (or one whom the master wished to shame) washed guests' feet.

When He had washed their feet . . . He said to them, "Do you know what I have done to you? You call Me Teacher and Lord, and you say well, for so I am. If I then, your Lord and Teacher, have washed your feet, you also ought to wash one another's feet. For I have given you an example, that you should do as I have done to you. Most assuredly, I say to you, a servant is not greater than his master; nor is he who is sent greater than he who sent him. If you know these things, happy are you if you do them (John 13:12-17).

That's the source of legitimate power: service and submission to others. Paul said, "For the commandments . . . are summed up in this saying, namely, 'You shall love your neighbor as yourself'" (Rom. 13:9).

Many leaders impose their power. Aspiring leaders yearn for power, and when they gain it they always want more.

Jesus taught the reverse. For Him, the way up is down. The way to become the master is to be the servant. The way to greatness is self-abnegation. The way to exaltation is to take up the cross daily and follow Him (Luke 9:23).

Power, Fear, and Love

In his sixteenth-century treatise entitled *The Prince,* Italian statesman and philosopher Niccolo Machiavelli argued for an absolute monarchy. He also asked a vital question— whether it is better to have a relationship based on love (as in personal power) or fear (as in position power). He stated that it works better to have both. But when one could not have both, he added, power ought to be based on fear; it tends to last longer, and those involved must pay a price to terminate the relationship. Love-based power, he said, tends to be short-lived and easily terminated since the follower feels no fear of retaliation.

Machiavelli put into words the guiding principle of many leaders. Yet Jesus the leader never resorted to exploiting fear. Instead, Jesus taught the overriding importance of love. On the night of His betrayal, while still in the Upper Room, He told His disciples:

A new commandment I give to you, that you love one another; as I have loved you, that you also love one another. By this all will know that you are My disciples, if you have love one for another (John 13:34-35).

In the first Letter of John, the apostle writes of both fear and love:

God is love, and he who abides in love abides in God, and God in him. Love has been among us . . . that we may have boldness in the Day of Judgment; because as He is, so are we in this world. There is no fear in love; but perfect love casts out fear, because fear involves torment (1 John 4:16-18).

Jesus derived His power from God. He exercised that power through love. He extended His power to His people, along with the best safeguard against its abuse: the commandment to love one another. If as a leader I love people, I will never try to manipulate or exploit them. I will keep their needs before me and do my best for them.

Two symbols of Christianity are the towel and the cross. The towel symbolizes service; the cross obedience. Both are marks of Christian leadership because they stand for Jesus' leadership style.

Many times Jesus could have used people for His purposes. Instead He led them to face themselves, as He did with the woman at the well, the woman taken in adultery, and Nicodemus. Once they looked at themselves, He revealed His love and redemptive power. That's how leadership with integrity works—using power to meet other's needs, not our own.

Thus we see our next leadership principle:

PRINCIPLE 10:
LEADERS RECEIVE THEIR GREATEST POWER TO OBEY GOD AND TO SERVE OTHERS.

CHAPTER ELEVEN

EGO

A well-known speaker who had appeared on many TV talk shows was invited to speak at a prestigious organization's annual gathering. The organizer of the event had phoned and later confirmed by mail how much the organization wanted him: "We're all anxious to meet you and to have you speak to us. You'd be amazed at how often our members quote you and how frequently they have suggested your name."

The day of the gathering arrived. The speaker arrived a few minutes early. He walked in, registered, and received a name tag, but no one paid any attention to him.

Less than five minutes before he was to speak, an announcement came over the public address system: "Has _____ arrived yet?"

Later the speaker confessed to me that his feelings had been hurt because no one had seemed to recognize him. "I wanted to walk out of the place," he said to me. "They had built me up before I came and let me down when I arrived." He had also found it hard to hold back the disappointment and anger when he spoke to the group.

The Ego of Jesus

Jesus never seemed upset when people didn't recognize Him. He usually avoided publicity and recognition.

In one instance, Philip urged Nathanael to come and meet Jesus (John 1:46-51). When Nathanael learned where Jesus had come from, he said, "Can anything good come out of Nazareth?" (v. 46)

Jesus never rebuked Nathanael for that. By now the Lord's fame had begun to spread through the land, but He showed no sign of being offended at not being recognized. He talked with Nathaniel, and when they finished Nathanael said, "You are the Son of God! You are the King of Israel!" (v. 49)

From His usual practice we can assume that Jesus had not blurted, "I am the Messiah!" He probably did not even hint at who He was. Jesus the leader concentrated on teaching, preaching, and demonstrating His purpose for coming. He allowed His audiences to discover His identity for themselves.

Wherever Jesus traveled, He expected no banners, no reception committee, no special honor. His ego did not seek the fulfillment which could have come had others worshiped Him or accorded Him titles of respect. As He said, "I do not receive honor from men" (5:41). He came with a mission and a message—point people to the Father—not to usurp another's position.

When the disciples offered Him food as He sat beside a well, Jesus said, "My food is to do the will of Him who sent Me, and to finish His work" (4:34). The cryptic remark did not mean so much that He wasn't hungry, but that His own needs were subordinated to the mission His Father had given Him. He exercised leadership over the disciples to point them toward accomplishing the Father's work too.

When we look at leadership today, we seldom see the non-egocentric style of Jesus. He came on a servant's mission; to do the Father's will—not to be a celebrity.

Leadership requires that men and women recognize what they have to do and work toward doing it. That sounds simplistic; yet many would-be-recognized leaders, instead of giving themselves to their work, dream of what they could do or will do one day. Or they keep expecting recognition for every achievement.

Even when individuals do put themselves into their work they expect appreciation. If some leaders do a good job for their company, they expect accolades. When overlooked, they either pout in private or angrily speak of their rights in public. They forget the example of Jesus Christ.

Getting the Credit

A Christian woman in a publishing house had a title of editorial assistant. She read manuscripts after her editor had finished them, checking mainly for grammatical and punctuation errors.

Her boss, an incompetent woman, realized the assistant had more ability than *she* did—and allowed the assistant to take over more and more of the actual editorial work. Eventually the assistant did most of the work, though the editor received the credit.

One day, in an argument with the publisher, the editor threatened to resign if a demand she'd made wasn't met. The publisher replied, "You might as well leave. Your assistant's been doing most of the work anyway."

"Did she tell you that?" the editor cried.

"She didn't need to," said the publisher. "I've been aware of it for months, wondering when you'd give her credit."

The end of this little true story is that the assistant editor eventually became the editor. She did her work well and did not expect acknowledgment. When the publisher, a non-Christian, asked her why she worked so hard yet never said anything about it, she quoted Colossians 3:23-24; "Whatever you do, do it heartily, as to the Lord and not to men, knowing that from the Lord you will receive the reward of your inheritance; for you serve the Lord Christ."

"I determined long ago not to seek glory for myself," she told her weekly Bible study group. "I'm ambitious, and I don't think there's anything displeasing to God about that. But I promised God I would never try to get ahead by undermining anyone else. When I realized what my boss was doing, I told God I would do the best work I knew how and leave the recognition up to Him."

Two years later, the publisher said to that lady, "I don't know much about religion, but I know one thing. If anyone in the world is a Christian, you are."

That's leadership—*true* leadership. It happens when people want to see the work done and they care little about who gets the credit.

Recognition: a Two-way Street

Competent leaders, because they have a sense of satisfaction and self-worth, want to recognize those who help them. They take no credit that belongs to someone else. When accepting recognition for their achievements, leaders carefully add, "But I couldn't have done it without the help of _____ ." They mean those words too.

Real leaders see themselves as part of a team. They don't seek ego rewards for themselves; yet if rewards come, they want to share the limelight with others.

A little limelight is OK. True leaders do not hide from

recognition. They do not show embarrassment by muttering, "Who, me? Why, I haven't done anything special." Those words often come from people who are feigning humility. I suspect they want *more* praise for their accomplishments and greater assurances of their worth.

One leader wisely said, "When I do a good job, I know it. Of course, I appreciate it when recognition comes to me. But I do my best because it's my job. I've committed myself and my work to God."

No matter what kind of leadership we exercise—standing in front of a worshiping congregation, guiding a family, directing sales efforts, or practicing law—as Christians we are serving Jesus Christ. Jesus said we will not receive glory from God if we receive it from people, and that if we perform only for the praise of others, we aren't working with the right motives. It is God's "well done" that we seek.

What happens when people don't see your work? What if they see it but don't appreciate it? Do you still keep going? Jesus could say yes. Not all of us could, because praise from people means too much to us.

The Secure Leader
When outstanding Christian leaders take on their roles, they tacitly promise to do their best for the church or company. They receive the position because someone or a committee thinks them capable; by accepting the responsibility, they agree to produce the desired results. Another way of saying this comes from the Apostle Paul, who wrote, "It is required in stewards that one be found faithful" (1 Cor. 4:2).

True leaders also have enough self-assurance or ego strength to know who they are and what they can do. They do not fear losing their positions. They don't naively allow unscrupulous people to take over, but don't worry about having their status taken away either. They have learned to follow the exhortation of Paul:

> Be anxious for nothing, but in everything by prayer and supplication, with thanksgiving, let your requests be made known to God; and the peace of God, which passes all understanding, will guard your hearts and minds through Christ Jesus (Phil. 4:6-7).

In one company the assistant manager had no peace. He watched anxiously whenever the manager called anyone into his office for more than a couple of minutes. Within the next hour the assistant would be at that person's desk, asking questions. He thought he asked subtly, but everyone knew he feared the manager would promise an employee something that might undermine his own position as assistant manager.

There is another ego-related quality typical of true Christian leaders. They have enough security in themselves and in their relationships with Jesus Christ that they don't have to compete with anyone else.

Can one be noncompetitive yet excellent? Yes! One of the best illustrations I can think of concerns the Mahre twins, Steve and Phil. They competed in the men's giant slalom event during the 1984 Winter Olympics in Sarajevo. As brothers they had naturally competed against each other all their lives. In the Olympic finals, Phil skied before his brother and held first place. When Steve's turn came, Phil got on the walkie-talkie and told his brother about problems to expect on the way down, especially slickness at the bottom. He spoke not as a competitor trying to hold onto his first-place position, but as a man who wanted to see his brother do his best. Steve came in second, and the twins stood side by side at the awards ceremony to receive the gold and silver medals.

When reporters asked Phil how he felt about winning, he said something like, "I was here to perform to the best of my ability. I am in the sport because I love it."

That attitude typifies real leaders. They earn their positions of leadership, but have no fear of others who might outshine them.

PRINCIPLE 11:
LEADERS WHO ARE SECURE IN JESUS CHRIST HAVE NOTHING TO PROTECT.

CHAPTER TWELVE

ANGER

A Muslim, to whom several Christians had talked about their faith, asked them a challenging question one day. "Why is it that when I yell at my children, you call it anger? If you Christians do it, you call it righteous indignation. What's the difference?"

I've heard the same question asked concerning Jesus' behavior in the temple when He threw out the money changers. We usually call Him righteously indignant, not just angry. What's the difference?

To find the answer, and to see what role anger should take in a leader's life, we need to examine the temple incident. John's Gospel records the story in 2:13-22. Even though John does not put a name on Jesus' feelings, the Lord was angry—and He showed it.

Turmoil in the Temple

Jesus did four things in the temple that day: He made whips, drove out the animals, poured the changers' money on the ground, and overturned the tables. Nowhere else in the recorded ministry of Jesus can we find Him showing such outward anger.

If we want to know why Jesus behaved as He did, we must understand the background of money changing in the temple. It begins with the fact that Passover was the greatest of all Jewish feasts; the Law stated that every Jewish male who lived within twenty miles of Jerusalem had to attend this observance. By the first century, Jews who had been scattered all over the world came back to their ancestral land for Passover. Scholars estimate that at least 2 million people assembled in Jerusalem for this event.

The Law required every male aged nineteen and above to pay a tax so that the priests could continue making temple sacrifices. They paid the tax in either Galilean shekels or "the shekels of the sanctuary," because all other coins were considered ceremonially unclean. Currency from other nations, though accepted for trade throughout Jerusalem, could not be used in worship to God. Since pilgrims came from all over the world with their own currency, money changers sat in the temple courts making the exchange for them.

Had their trade been honest, the money changers would have been doing an honorable job. But they charged exorbitantly for the changing of coins; scholars estimate this business brought in $200,000 a year.

Sellers of animals also set up their shops in the temple. The Law allowed only *perfect* birds and animals to be sacrificed, so when inspectors examined animals the worshipers brought in, they naturally declared the creatures flawed. This forced the people to buy other animals at outrageous prices.

These two injustices would have been bad enough on the world's terms. But perpetrated in the name of religion, and with the obvious consent of the religious leaders, they became even more repellent.

Jesus became angry at what He saw going on in the temple. The merchants had desecrated God's house. They had made money dishonorably from many who could ill afford to pay.

So He chased them out. Why? To show them that the temple was to be a house of prayer. Mark 11:17 reads, "My house shall be called a house of prayer for all nations." The buying and selling apparently went on in the Court of the Gentiles—the only place non-Jews could enter. If Gentiles searching for God had wanted to pray or meditate, they would have had no place to go. The area was in a constant uproar of oxen, sheep, doves, and tradesmen.

It is also possible that Jesus wanted to make it known that animal sacrifices no longer pleased God. We can see how God viewed the sacrifices in passages such as Isaiah 1:11, 13: "I have had enough of burnt offerings of rams and the fat of fed cattle. I do not delight in the blood of bulls, or of lambs or goats. . . . Bring no more futile sacrifices." Other Old Testament passages, including Jeremiah 7:22; Hosea 5:6; and Psalm 51:16 say much the same thing.

Jesus showed anger that day. Call it righteous anger if you must, but not mere indignation.

Other References to Anger

One other incident in Jesus' life clearly showed His ability to become angry. A man wanted Jesus to heal him on the Sabbath. The Jewish leaders watched because if He healed the man, He would be doing "work"—and they could condemn Him under the Law. Mark 3:5 states, "When He [Jesus] had looked around at them with anger, being grieved by the hardness of their hearts, He said to the man, 'Stretch out your hand.' " Despite opposition, He healed the man.

In neither of these incidents did God seem displeased with His Son's actions. Nowhere in the Bible, in fact, does God ever condemn anyone simply for being angry. He may condemn us for actions we take in anger; if our anger results in harm or cruelty, we have clearly sinned. But the ability to become angry is a trait of God Himself.

Several times the Old Testament speaks of God's anger: Deuteronomy 1:37; 4:21; 9:8, 20; 1 Kings 8:46; Psalm 2:12; 79:5, 85:5; Isaiah 12:1. Paul separates anger from sin in Ephesians 4:26: "If you become angry, do not let your anger lead you into sin; and do not stay angry all day" (GNB).

Nowhere does the Bible say we must not get angry. Paul exhorts that those elected to the office of bishop must not be "soon angry." I take that to mean they should not be short-tempered people. It is normal for Christians, including leaders, to become angry. As a friend told me, "Only two kinds of people never get angry: those physically dead and those emotionally dead." But for Jesus' followers, it must be the right *kind* of anger.

Healthy Anger

Healthy anger—aimed at injustice, wrong doing and evil—is proper in its place. Here are examples:

● In 1981 an organization called MADD (Mothers Against Drunk Drivers) began in the United States because a mother, Candy Lightner, lost a teenaged daughter when a drunk driver ran into her. Mrs. Lightner communicated her anger to other parents who had lost sons and daughters in similar ways, and MADD soon boomed into a national movement.

● Anger at child abuse has brought the problem to the attention of many who never considered it before. Now a greater effort is being made to stop abuse and counsel those who were abused as children.

● Angry, humiliated women have let the world know that rape is an act of violence, not passion, and that they have not provoked men into attacking them. A new determination to wipe out such violence is spreading.

● Anger over drug abuse has raised up fighters who want to stop drug traffic and help people free themselves from addiction. The problem is far from solved but some progress has been made.

Many reform moments have begun because courageous people became angry—angry enough to take corrective measures. Consider the blazing anger of two antislavery champions—Harriet Beecher Stowe writing *Uncle Tom's Cabin* on one side of the Atlantic, and William Wilberforce making fiery speeches on the other. As John Wesley said, "Give me a hundred men who fear nothing but God, and who hate nothing but sin, and who know nothing but Jesus Christ and Him crucified, and I will shake the world."

Unhealthy Anger

Most of us are not so noble with our anger. Our displeasure shows itself in unloving ways, and our "indignation" is not exactly righteous. We become angry for reasons like these:

● We are frustrated. This habit begins with temper tantrums in early childhood, but doesn't end there.

● We are anxious. We perceive a threat to ourselves, to our possessions, or to our loved ones.

● We don't like ourselves or feel we have failed. Often our anger is turned inward and becomes depression.

● We are (or think we are) unjustly treated. Something happens that we feel is not "right."

Most of us are probably not satisfied with the way we handle anger. Some are by nature more volatile than others, ready to battle at the drop of an unkind word or deed. Others remind me of smoldering leaves; their fire builds under the surface until an incident sends the flame out of control. Regardless of our type, we must learn how to handle anger for the benefit of ourselves and those we lead. Leaders certainly aren't the only humans prone to anger, but our roles can present us with unusual stress—and ensure that the "fallout" will affect others if we "blow up."

Handling Anger

The first step to handling anger is admitting responsibility for our reactions. That may sound like a minor point, but I know many who will acknowledge that they cannot control their tempers—and then give every excuse in the book for noncontrol:

- "I'm a redhead, and that tells you I've got a temper."
- "I'm Italian (or Spanish or whatever), and we're all hot-blooded."
- "My whole family is angry."
- "I like to let people know where I stand. I believe in telling it like it is, even if somebody has to get hurt in the process."

The second step toward control is to understand what anger does to us. Physical changes occur when we get angry, because our bodies prepare for a fight. Adrenaline pours into our systems; blood pressure increases, hearts beat faster. Blood even clots more quickly than normal, in case we are injured while acting out our anger. The pupils of our eyes dilate, our muscles tense, and our digestive tracts can become so spastic that we feel abdominal pains.

Anger, in short, mobilizes us for action. But because the causes of our anger seldom require a fistfight, much of that tension is likely to be held inside us—often causing long-range physical problems. Thus we usually do ourselves no favor by "getting mad." Realizing that can motivate us to react less extremely.

A third step toward healthy anger is to think again of the story of Jesus cleansing the temple. He was angry and took action. But He controlled His anger, directing it toward one end: getting rid of things that desecrated the temple.

That's one characteristic of good anger: it is carefully directed. Unrestrained anger that lashes out at anything and everything is not part of the leadership style of Jesus.

Good anger also directs itself without malice or hatred. When Jesus cleansed the temple He took drastic action, but we find nothing to indicate that He hated the people involved.

Finally, good anger shows itself in corrective measures. Good anger directs itself against problems, not people. Most of us have heard the old saying, "Love the sinner, hate the sin." That's how good anger operates. It makes no attacks on the value of individuals, but attacks their wrong actions.

This does not mean, however, that we should deny the anger we feel. Too many leaders, especially Christians, attempt to repress anger. Or they'll acknowledge only, "I was miffed," or "It troubled me." But we can hold only so much anger inside before it will spill out, often at the most inappropriate times.

With God's help, keeping in mind the example of Jesus, we can control the "temperature" of our reactions and direct our anger into healthy channels. When we do, it can make us better people and more effective leaders.

PRINCIPLE 12:
LIKE JESUS, TRUE LEADERS EXPRESS ANGER IN HEALTHY WAYS.

4 Part

THE PROBLEMS OF LEADERSHIP

CHAPTER THIRTEEN

THE SEARCH FOR SUPPORT

When someone seriously considers running for political office, he or she attempts to find out how much public support such a candidacy would arouse. When people start a new business, they have to ask early, "Will people buy our product? How much of a market can we expect to get?" When I decided to write this book, I had to answer two questions, because I knew any good editor would ask them anyway: (1) Who will read this book? (2) Would enough people buy the book to make it worth a publisher's efforts and resources?

Research is a prerequisite to starting anything new in business or politics today. That applies to churches too. When a denomination decides to plant churches in a new area, research is used to determine whether enough potential members live there.

But when God sent Jesus Christ, He did not seem to make statistics a matter of consideration. Jesus didn't send out twelve marketing experts to stand on street corners and ask, "If God sent His Messiah to you, would you support Him, follow Him, and pledge yourself unconditionally to Him?"

Jesus as PR Man

In some ways Jesus made things hard for Himself. Public relations experts would probably point out five serious mistakes He made. First, He did not go to the upper-class members of Jewish society. That would have been the logical starting place because they had influence, power, and resources. Second, He wasted time by going to the opposite extreme and calling on the poor, the sick, the tax collectors, shepherds, and the not-so-very-nice people. Third, He didn't try to talk people into supporting His messiahship. He had no sales pitch, made no glorious promises. Fourth, He alienated those in leadership. It was bad enough that He didn't start with the top echelon, but at times it seemed He went out of His way to confront them. Fifth, He refused to compromise. All leaders know that no matter how lofty their ideals, they can't have everything. They give up a few nonessential demands, and in return receive a lot of fringe benefits, endorsements, and political favors.

Had there been an election in the first century in and around Jerusalem, trying to choose a Saviour, not many people would have voted for Jesus. In the end He didn't have a lot of popular appeal.

But for Jesus, other things meant more than popular appeal. We stake so much on having a good reputation, being appreciated, and garnering all the platitudes, plaques, and awards we can, but He usually stood alone.

Jesus did His own thing whether or not anyone supported Him. In an incident recorded at the end of John 6, the Lord had spoken strongly to would-be followers and let them know what it mwant to follow. Except for a handful of diehards, everyone left. Jesus finally asked, "Do you also want to go away?" (6:67)

Peter hurriedly answered, "Lord, to whom shall we go? You have the words of eternal life. Also we have come to believe and know that You are the Christ, the Son of the living God" (6:68-69).

The disciples stayed. But what if all of them had left? What would Jesus have done? My own guess is that while it would have saddened Jesus, He still would have continued His ministry. He had come to save humankind, with or without human support.

Leaders without Followers

Sometimes leaders and visionaries find themselves alone, without support, because of their own problems or mistakes. They turn people away with their attitudes or behavior and then feel sorry for themselves as they "suffer for the Lord."

One Christian, for instance, had an idea to help people earn money and get the Gospel out at the same time. He started to make products printed with Bible verses and inspirational thoughts. When he contacted friends and acquaintances, more than fifty people invested in his organization to the tune of at least $1,000 each. His graphs and charts showed how investors would make at least 18 percent interest after the first two years. He planned to sell more stock and eventually distribute his wares all over the United States and Canada, then overseas.

But the Securities and Exchange Commission, a federal regulatory agency, notified him that he had violated laws in the way he issued and sold stock. Instead of attempting to get things straightened out, he continued as he had in the past. "Just government interference," he said. Finally the government stopped him from selling any more stock and charged him with a number of irregularities and violations.

Eventually all the investors lost every cent they had loaned the man. Later he went around complaining, "The government is against anyone who wants to do God's work," and "As soon as you start trying to do something great for God, the devil puts up a battle." But he had brought the problems on himself.

At other times, however, a leader's lack of support isn't his own fault. Jesus' vision came from God; He knew what He was doing. He understood His mission and was determined to carry it out. Had He listened to people around Him, He never would have accomplished anything.

"Wait a minute," you might say. "We can look at the style of Jesus, understand His principles, and follow His example—up to a point. But there's a big difference between Jesus and me. He is sinless. He always knew what He should do, so He didn't have to worry about getting others' support."

That's right. We still have human imperfection at work in us, no matter how far we have progressed in the Christian life. We still wrestle with problems like pride, self-esteem, rejection, defensiveness, and insecurity. When we find ourselves at odds with others, we can never be fully certain that we have been totally honest and faithful to God—and that others are opposing Him by opposing us.

As a friend of mine says, "Our motives, at best, are mixed." He points out that sin blinds, hides, and deceives: "How can I truly know what's in my heart? Even when God speaks, my sinful nature sometimes affects my hearing."

Guidelines for Lonely Leaders

So what *can* you do to sort out your motives when you want to lead in a new direction but face opposition?

- Seek guidance from God. Ask Him to show you whether this direction is right for you. Test your plans against His Word.
- Share your concern with a few trusted Christian friends. Ask them to pray with and for you.
- Search your own heart. Do you have peace about your plans? Do you have a sense that this pleases God? Do you feel anger toward those who oppose you? If God wants you to engage in a new business or activity, He will give you peace, despite the opposition of others.

One couple I know followed these three steps. They believed God wanted them to go as missionaries to Africa, despite violent political upheavals there. Their families tried to dissuade them, especially since the couple had three preschool children. A mission board finally accepted them —but with reluctance, and only after the would-be missionaries had faced oppostion at every turn.

The husband told a prayer-support group, "I had such an inner assurance from God that it didn't matter if no one supported me. I knew God was with me, and we determined to go."

They did. They spent several years of outstanding ministry in Africa. Had they listened to opposing voices, they would never have gone. God's peace made the difference.

Never Alone at the Top

After the Apostle Paul traveled across most of the Jewish world, God wanted him to go to Rome. But every time Paul talked to Christians, they opposed the trip. The Prophet Agabus warned him of the dangers, saying he would be imprisoned. The brethren pleaded with Paul, trying to persuade him to turn back.

This was Paul's response: "What do you mean by weeping

and breaking my heart? For I am ready not only to be bound, but also to die at Jerusalem for the name of the Lord Jesus" (Acts 21:13).

The next verse says, "And when he [Paul] would not be persuaded, we ceased, saying, 'The will of the Lord be done.'"

Sometimes a leader must stand alone, humanly speaking. When he or she feels the guidance of God in a direction, has taken every precaution to check out God's will, and still persists in saying, "This is the right thing for me," he or she must do it. Sometimes that means doing it alone—with no one's help but God's, that is.

After we surrender our lives to Jesus Christ, we are never really alone. The psalmist wrote, "When my father and my mother forsake me, then the Lord will take care of me" (Ps. 27:10). Those words probably refer to more than literal parents. Likely it means, "Even if everyone forsakes me, even my own parents. . . ."

From outward appearances, Jesus stood alone. His disciples wanted Him to declare His power, to overthrow the Romans, to destroy the wicked. They didn't understand Jesus' mission or methods, and when He was arrested they ran away in fear or denied Him. Even then Jesus stood fast—with His Father.

A Singular Challenge
Christian leadership, like discipleship, carries no guarantees that anyone will understand us. Our commitment to God never assures us encouragement from any human source. The greater our vision, the more we may have to stand utterly without human support.

Others have done it before us. Men and women have dreamed great dreams and seen them come true despite obstacles and opposition.

One man who held on to his dream is S. Truett Cathy. In 1966 he started a restaurant in Hapeville, on the south side of Atlanta, specializing in hamburgers and what later became known as fast foods. A few years later he opened another restaurant in nearby Forest Park, Georgia.

Everything was going well and profits were coming in, when one day the Forest Park restaurant burned down. Insurance covered only a small part of the cost, but Truett rebuilt the restaurant. This time, aware of the trend toward more fast foods, he designed it for that market. The only problem was that Truett was ahead of his time; within three months the rebuilt restaurant had all but failed.

Did he give up? No—because he had a vision of what he could do. He had been experimenting with cooking chicken and believed he had developed the best-tasting chicken sandwich in the world. Despite pessimistic voices around him, he persisted. Today he is the president of Chick-fil-A, with well over 300 restaurants in over 30 American states.

Then there was another man. He was shy, afraid of people, and stumbled over words when he spoke. But he had a zeal for God and worked hard at any job the pastor or board asked him to do.

One day this man felt God call him into the ministry. His pastor and church board, who loved him and appreciated his willingness to do anything they asked, gave him reluctant approval as he left for ministerial training. On the day the young man left I stood next to the church treasurer, who said to me, "It seems like such a shame for him to waste three years of training, because he'll never make it as a minister." I agreed.

Three years later the young man came back and preached at our church. None of us could believe he was the same person. He had developed poise, his message flowed; he was a first-class preacher.

I asked him what had happened to him during that three-year period. He said he had kept on praying, and telling God, "I believe You want me to do this. I'm doing everything I know to be Your servant. You do what You have to do to make me into a good one."

One man alone with God, became a superb preacher. Only those of us who had known him in his younger days can truly appreciate the great work that God has done in his life.

That principle can work in all our lives. Here is one way to put it:

PRINCIPLE 13:
ONE TRUE LEADER WITH GOD'S HELP EQUALS A STRONG MAJORITY.

CHAPTER FOURTEEN

DOUBTERS

Jesus' style of leadership was distinguished by its ability to deal with a variety of temperaments, conditions, and levels of spiritual maturity. After His resurrection, for example, He displayed this ability in brilliant fashion.

That was when He dealt with Mary the loyalist, Peter the penitent, the two thinkers on the way to Emmaus, and Thomas the doubter. Jesus' leadership was sufficient for all these conditions, curing, reconciling, assuring, and giving hope.

Of all those Jesus faced after His resurrection, Thomas was perhaps the toughest challenge. Thomas was out when Jesus appeared to the disciples, so he missed this opportunity to see the risen Lord. The doubter called his fellow disciples liars because he did not believe their word. He arrogantly assumed the right to lay down conditions on which he would believe.

We can see in Thomas not only a doubter but also a constitutional pessimist. When Jesus talked about going to Bethany after Lazarus' death, Thomas' reaction was, "Let us also go, that we may die with Him" (John 11:16). He saw only the dark side of the truth.

Often leaders are called on to deal with such people—executives, church members, or family members who cannot see any good in themselves, their situations, or the leader's plans. These people are often gloomy as well as doubters. They can't trust anybody or anything.

Like Thomas, many of these people have preconceived ideas and are unwilling to change. They demand evidence which is difficult or impossible to provide. The leader's word is often not good enough for such people; they must see it to believe it.

Martin Luther said, "The art of doubting is easy." Perhaps that's because we are born with this tendency. Some of us work to minimize that side of our nature; others feed it, and it grows. If it keeps growing, our other side—trust—will gradually wither away.

Conversely, if we starve doubt and feed trust, doubt will gradually fade away. When trust is present, doubt goes; when trust goes, doubt returns.

When doubt sets in between workers and bosses, everything is suspect. Every late start is counted; every request for time off is viewed with skepticism; every idea presented is rejected out of hand. When doubt comes between husband and wife, every conversation seems to turn into an argument. Words are misunderstood or twisted. The result can be disastrous.

The Arabs have a saying: "Your beloved will swallow the gravel for you, but your enemy will count your every error." So will one who doubts you.

Doubt is the root of most strife in our churches, businesses, homes, and governments. It is the root of unbelief. Doubts about God make people unwilling to submit to His authority.

How Leaders Deal with Doubt

How did Jesus deal with Thomas, His doubting follower? We need to examine not only the psychology of Jesus' response, but also His spiritual leadership.

It was a long week between the Resurrection and the following Sunday. On the surface it would seem much kinder if Jesus hadn't left the disciples for the whole week with their newfound, tremulous, raw conviction.

But on a deeper level, by leaving them to reflect for a week, Jesus allowed their spiritual growth to be considered. New thoughts, new vision needed time to be molded into the lives of the disciples.

So they were left to quiet reflection, to meditation, to adjust their thoughts, to start to understand. As a mother stands a few feet from her toddler to encourage him to try to walk, Jesus left them alone to experiment with that self-reliance and God-reliance which was to become their permanent condition.

And then He came back. This time He did not concern Himself so much with the group, but singled out the doubter—the one who had set down conditions for trusting. Jesus did not do what leaders are often inclined to do; He did not speak to the whole group attacking doubt in general, hoping that the doubter would get the message. Nor did He surround Himself with "yes men," leaving out the doubters, hoping that doubters would get the message and leave.

That would not reflect the leadership style of Jesus. His solution was to concentrate on the doubter, repeating—then meeting—the doubter's demands.

Can you imagine the shame, embarrassment, and brokenness Thomas must have felt when Jesus quoted to him his own demand to touch the Lord's wounds as a condition of belief? How different they must have sounded coming out of Jesus' mouth.

There is no surer way to make a person ashamed of his or her wild words than to repeat them when the person is cool and calm. Christ granting Thomas' request was a sharp rebuke of the request, as well as a path to reconciliation and belief.

Jesus gave Thomas a warning: "Do not be unbelieving, but believing" (John 20:27). In one sense Jesus was saying, "It is not a matter of evidence, Thomas, it is a question of disposition. Your incredulity is not due to a lack of evidence, but to your tendency and attitude." To put it another way, there is enough light in the sun: it is our eyes that grow dim. Deep under the problem of doubt lies the problem of disposition and attitude.

From Doubt to Belief

Jesus' style of leadership always aimed at reforming, encouraging, and moving people from one point of their lives to a higher point; from doubt to belief, from skepticism to commitment, from enmity to love. In other words, He helped people grow.

Jesus did not deal with individuals in order to shame them or show off, though He had every right to. He did not face doubters personally merely to show them how wrong they were. He wanted people to move toward their God-given potentials.

As Nathanael had exclaimed when he knew Jesus had seen him under the fig tree, "Rabbi, You are the Son of God!" (John 1:49) so Thomas forgets his incredulity and breaks into a rapturous confession: "My Lord and my God!" (John 20:28)

So swiftly did Thomas' attitude change that it leaves us without a doubt that Jesus' strategy worked. The result He sought was the spiritual growth of those who doubted Him.

This too is His leadership style.

PRINCIPLE 14:
TRUE LEADERS HELP DOUBTERS GROW INTO TRUSTERS.

CHAPTER FIFTEEN

CRITICISM

I walked into an office one day and saw these words on a sign on the manager's desk:

To avoid criticism:
Say nothing. Do nothing. Be nothing.

I'm not sure even *that* works. In fact, I can't figure out *any* way to avoid criticism, especially as a leader.

Most of us struggle with how to receive criticism. It's hard enough to take when it's justified. But when it's unjust, unkind, or done in such a way that we hear it from a third party with no opportunity to defend or explain, it's worse.

None of us is immune to criticism. Here is one volley aimed at a well-known figure:

He is no better than a murderer. He is treacherous in private friendships, a hypocrite in public life, an impostor who has either abandoned all good principles or else never had any.

That comment referred to President George Washington. About another chief executive, a newspaper editorial writer said:

The President is a low, cunning clown. He is the original gorilla. Those who seek the apeman are fools to travel all the way to Africa when what they want can be readily found in Springfield, Illinois.

Those remarks referred to Abraham Lincoln. If the likes of Washington and Lincoln can be so severely criticized, it's no wonder that leaders like ourselves come in for our share of complaints.

Critics of Jesus

Jesus never escaped His detractors either. Those who criticized Him did so for a variety of reasons including jealousy, hatred, and fear. When He debated some Jewish leaders, for example, they said, "You have a demon" (John 7:20). Today's secular critics would probably make that, "You are a paranoid schizophrenic and need to be locked up."

A revealing statement appears in John 15:25: "But this happened that the Word might be fulfilled which is written in their Law, 'They hated Me without a cause.'" Jesus' critics had no real cause to hate Him. Many did not understand Him, but many made no effort to understand. They rejected anyone who tried to change anything, and Jesus was a changer.

I've always wondered how people could see the evidence of Jesus' healing and compassion at work and still speak against Him. But they did. As mentioned in chapter 6, Jesus healed a man by the pool called Bethesda (John 5:1-16). When the religious leaders saw that the man who had been crippled for thirty-eight years, was now healed, they didn't rejoice. They criticized Jesus for healing on the Sabbath. "For this reason the Jews persecuted Jesus, and sought to kill Him, because He had done these things on the Sabbath" (John 5:16).

(134)

On another Sabbath Jesus healed a man who had been born blind. "Some of the Pharisees said, 'This Man is not from God, because He does not keep the Sabbath' " (John 9:16).

During the Feast of Tabernacles, the people argued among themselves about Jesus. Some knew of His works and openly spoke of His power and goodness. "And there was much murmuring among the people concerning Him. Some said, 'He is good'; others said, 'No, on the contrary, He deceives the people' " (John 7:12).

When religious leaders captured Jesus, they brought Him to Pilate. When Pilate asked the charges they replied, "If He were not an evildoer, we would have not delivered Him up to you" (John 18:30).

Strange isn't it, that they didn't list His "crimes"? Apparently Pilate did not insist. The Lord's accusers represented the godly of their day; on their word and reputations they brought Jesus for punishment and death.

That type of criticism against Christianity never changed. Even as the Book of Acts closed, the Apostle Paul visited leaders in Rome and wanted to talk to them about Jesus. They agreed to listen but said, "For concerning this sect, we know that it is spoken against everywhere" (Acts 28:22). The story records that some believed, many did not. I suspect that the nonbelievers had already made up their minds—like the people who brought Jesus to Pilate.

Handling Criticism
Criticism didn't seem to trouble Jesus. Perhaps because He knew the wickedness of human hearts He expected it. But most of us have a difficult time with it, especially when the criticism comes from other believers.

A friend who taught a Sunday School class of nearly 300 adults once attracted a barrage of criticism. He confided, "I expect people outside the church to criticize me. But it sure hurts when your brothers and sisters in Christ do it! It hurts even worse when they tell someone else who comes to me and lets me know."

This man had received flak for speaking up against the careless use of pesticides, especially DDT. This was years before most people realized how badly DDT upset the balance of nature. He had broached the subject when the class studied Genesis, saying that God gave Adam, and by inference his children throughout human history, the responsibility to take care of His world. It took years before the man's critics were proven wrong.

On the other hand, some criticism may be on target. The Apostle Paul knew that any leader needs to be open to other voices. So he went to Jerusalem with Barnabas and Titus, "and communicated to them that Gospel which I preach among the Gentiles, but privately to those who were of reputation, lest by any means I might run, or had run, in vain" (Gal. 2:2).

Paul had begun to preach that the Gospel frees us from the Law of Moses. That new and daring concept had not been proclaimed by others. Naturally he received a lot of criticism, so he stood before the leaders of God's church to explain it; they supported him.

It would have been impossible, of course, for Paul to run to Jerusalem every time he was criticized. He wrote to the Corinthians, "With me it is a very small thing that I should be judged by you or by a human court. . . . He who judges me is the Lord" (1 Cor. 4:3-4). This was not arrogance, but a moratorium on fighting and criticism. Paul did what he believed to be right, and knew that God would be his ultimate judge.

CRITICISM

First Response
What should be our first response to criticism? As Christian leaders we need to *listen*. Our critics may speak the truth. They may not do it with delicacy or tact, but truth is still truth no matter how it comes to us.

As Abraham Lincoln said when told that his Secretary of State had called him a fool, "Stanton is a wise man. If he said I am a fool, then I had better look into the matter."

When critics assail, most of us tend to flare up, get ready for verbal retort, or feel like crying. We want to defend ourselves, explain how unjust people are, or wail because others don't understand us. Instead we should listen.

Second Response
When criticism is justified, we need to correct whatever we can. We can only know its correctness if we search our hearts, pray for God to guide us, ask Him to open us to hear clearly, and seek the counsel of others.

If, having done all that, we believe the criticism is wrong, we need to ask God for the grace to bear the opposition. Some of us do that better than others. In our own strength few of us can throw off unfair criticism without a lot of inner turmoil.

After all, we want people to like us, to approve of us. We may even *expect* others' approval. When people respond to us negatively, we find ourselves hurt.

A business friend, for example, told me that in the 1950s he did business with both black people and white people. Many whites criticized him for treating blacks as equals. He told me that he never argued with the racists, figuring his actions wuld speak more eloquently than words. "But sometimes I had to do a heap of praying not to let my temper get riled because of those bigoted attitudes," he admitted.

Sometimes we can remind ourselves that, as the Apostle Paul said, "He who judges me is the Lord." If we know that we are putting God first in our lives, and have used the checks and balances already mentioned, we don't have to waste precious time defending ourselves against our critics.

Third Response

Finally, we need to prepare for criticism yet to come. If we know people will speak against us, belittle us, tear us down, we can build ourselves up and fortify ourselves against their charges.

One executive secretary has learned to cope with criticism. She keeps a printed prayer on the corner of her desk, next to her telephone. Since she receives most of the complaints directed at her company, she reads her prayer silently several times as she listens to the often angry callers. The prayer reads:

> Lord Jesus, You felt the hatred of sinners, and You loved them. Help me to remember that You can help me to love those who criticize me.

The Vocal Minority

Criticism often comes to leaders from a vocal minority. Yet they speak so loudly and so often that it's often hard to know how many people they represent.

One pastor made a lot of changes in his congregation. As a result the church grew for the first time in ninety years. Soon two morning services had to be held to accommodate people, and then additional classrooms and worship space had to be built.

About this time the pastor began to hear a lot of criticism.

It usually came to him through a member who started with, "They're saying. . . ."

One day, quite dispirited, the pastor paced back and forth in his office, wondering whether he ought to resign. He couldn't seem to think of any good he had done, how he had helped the church to grow, or how lives had been changed. He could only feel the criticism. The comments had become so hostile that he felt most of the people in the church were against him.

He wrote to a friend, "It's a terrible situation when you have over 400 members and 350 hate you. The other 50 don't care."

Then, in his anguish, he stopped and knelt. He prayed for peace of mind and guidance. Later he explained what happened next: "Almost immediately I realized that the complaints that filled my mind had come from four families—the power structure of the congregation before I became pastor—and they didn't want any change for any reason. I also realized that they represented a minority of the congregation."

We have to hear the critical voices, but we also have to put them in perspective. We might think from reading the persecution and criticism Jesus underwent that everyone opposed Him. Yet Mark says, "The common people heard Him gladly" (Mark 12:37).

The critical voices may have been loud, even murderous, but they came from the clique of religious leaders who didn't want Jesus to change things. Common people heard, rejoiced over, and embraced the teachings of Jesus Christ and His disciples.

When you encounter criticism, ask yourself a few questions before you allow yourself to be thrown into emotional turmoil:

- Where does the criticism come from?

- Is *everyone* against me? Or is it only a few malcontents?
- Is there truth in the criticism—even a little?
- Is there someting I need to learn from my critics' remarks?

Lyle Schaller, a longtime observer of churches and denominations, once reminded a group of church leaders that some people will always complain. These people have a whole bag of criticisms ready when a new program is suggested:

- It's too noisy.
- It's too worldly.
- It's too expensive.
- It's poor stewardship of God's money.
- It will attract the wrong kind of people.

But there are others who care about a program, he added. Listen to them. Don't stop an activity that fifty people want because three people start criticizing.

A friend told me, "Maybe you ought to feel good when people criticize you." That didn't make any sense to me, so I asked him what he meant.

He answered by quoting the words of Jesus: "Blessed are you when they revile and persecute you, and say all kinds of evil against you falsely for My sake. Rejoice and be exceedingly glad, for great is your reward in heaven, for so they persecuted the prophets who were before you" (Matt. 5:11-12).

Just before Jesus went to the Garden of Gethsemane, He said, "Remember the word that I said to you, 'A servant is not greater than his master.' If they persecuted Me, they will also persecute you. If they kept My word, they will keep yours also" (John 15:20).

When criticism is deserved, learn from it. When it is unjust, remember our next principle:

PRINCIPLE 15:
ONLY ONE LEADER WAS PERFECT, AND THEY CRITICIZED HIM TOO.

CHAPTER SIXTEEN

MOLEHILLS AND MOUNTAINS

A Christian leader left an organization after less than six months. He had produced outstanding results before joining that organization, and later proved himself capable with a new company. A friend introduced me to him, amd while we were chatting my friend asked him, "Why did you leave the _____ organization?"

"I can put it in one word," he said. "Pettiness." He didn't go into a harangue or mention personalities, but said something like, "They had no sense of teamwork. Everybody had to win over everybody else. Petty jealousies and rivalries were everywhere. Everybody tried to build a kingdom and then take control over the next kingdom. I wanted to work with everybody. After six months, no matter how much I tried not to get into the rivalry, if I cooperated with one person, I automatically showed my opposition to another. I decided to leave."

Petty problems seem small—and they are—but they also lower morale and productivity. Major problems such as financial survival are usually easy to recognize, but petty problems slide by almost unnoticed. Ignoring them eventually leads to problems of gigantic proportions.

Petty People

Here are a few of the petty leaders who, by their attitudes and working styles, bring conflict:

- *Promises-Promises.* "You want anything, just ask." He means it too—at least right now. Ten minutes from now he may have forgotten it.
- *Seven-Famous-Last-Words.* In any church or other organization, the "seven famous last words" are "We never tried it that way before." This petty person loves to go into endless detail explaining how something similar was tried twelve years ago and failed.
- *First-Thing-Tomorrow.* This classic procrastinator always seems busy, has no time to do anything extra, and never seems to get anything done on time. "When do you want it?" he's always asking. "I'll have it ready for you first thing tomorrow."
- *Opposing-Others'-Ideas.* This person has a lot of ideas, plenty of energy, and is always supporting new programs—as long as she comes up with the original idea. She has little use for ideas that originate elsewhere.
- *What's-in-It-for Me?* He withholds support, interest, and energy until he knows what he's going to get for his effort. If he's sophisticated enough, he manipulates conversation so that his aloofness comes out sounding like the most logical way to be. But no matter how it sounds, he has only one interest—himself.

Dozens of other petty types exist, including the cynic, the gossip, the self-appointed expert, the insensitive person, and the joker.

Petty people as problems can become so pervasive that they divert leaders from coping with serious difficulties. Haven't we all known of churches that argue over such issues as what color to paint the new kitchen, or whether to install pews or theater-type chairs for worship? They keep so stirred up on side issues that they neglect the real tasks of the church. The same can be true of businesses and even families.

Common Responses to Petty Problems

How do organizations usually handle these deceptively minor problems?

1. *Ignore them.* This is the most common method. Leaders don't see them or consider them too insignificant.

2. *Avoid them.* Leaders may recognize the problem and even admit that, unless corrected, it has the potential to cause great harm. But they say in effect, "If we work around it, it might go away." Unfortunately, allowing it to go unchecked gives the problem time, energy, and even encouragement to grow.

3. *Defuse them.* This tactic acknowledges conflict and offers delay. It asks people to cool down and promises that the leadership will struggle with the problem at a later time.

This can be useful. Leaders may say, "We'll come back to this one," and declare a moratorium for the time being. But the promise to solve the problem later musn't be forgotten.

4. *Resolve them.* Effective leaders attempt to resolve petty conflicts before they grow. They don't use a cannon when a pistol would work, but they note minor differences and reconcile the parties before chasms develop.

How Jesus Handled Petty Problems

In John 21:21 a petty problem comes to the surface. Jesus has just implied that Peter would one day die as a martyr. Peter sees John and asks, "But, Lord, what about this man?"

Peter's question about John's role in the work of God may have had a touch of jealousy in it. Peter was devoted to Christ, yet John was known as "the disciple whom Jesus loved," so a rivalry may have existed between the two. The question might also have shown a natural interest in John's fate. Would he be as important as Peter in terms of future leadership of the work? Should Peter have John accompany him? Was there something special in store for John?

Jesus answered, "If I will that he remain till I come, what is that to you? You follow Me" (John 21:22). This statement gently rebukes any evil that may have been in Peter's question. It warns against trying to force other people into the same groove or demanding "equal" treatment in the Lord's service. Jesus asked Peter to leave John alone and to concentrate on his own ministry.

In any organization or church, nothing squashes rumors, jealousies, and gossip like nipping them in the bud. To leave things to speculation can be the most dangerous condition in a group. Still Jesus did not say to Peter, "I have this in mind for John, but you must keep it in confidence." He did not ask, "What do you think I should do with John?" These responses would have puffed Peter up, magnified his ego, and caused further problems. Jesus struck a balance between encouraging speculation and divulging information that needed to be kept hidden.

It can also be seen in this passage that Jesus' style of leadership was not "divide to rule." He sought to minimize the potential conflict between Peter and John not exploit it. Creating dependence through division has been the style of imperialistic political powers, and even some past missionary endeavors. Some pastors feel that their survival depends on keeping factions pitted against each other; some company presidents and political leaders do too, not only to ensure their supremacy but because they don't trust their subordinates. Their institutions are constantly in a state of turmoil—and when things work smoothly, these leaders may create problems just to show they are needed to provide solutions!

Petty Problems in the Early Church

Rivalry and small nettling issues didn't stop with the ascension of Jesus Christ. The church, even in its early days, had to cope with such difficulties.

As recorded in the Book of Acts, the church fostered a communal atmosphere and provided for widows and orphans. Immediately problems faced the apostles, who had learned their leadership skills under Jesus Christ:

> Now in those days, when the number of the disciples was multiplying, there arose a murmuring against the Hebrews by the Hellenists, because their widows were neglected in the daily distribution. Then the Twelve summoned the multitude of the disciples and said, "It is not desirable that we should leave the Word of God and serve tables. Therefore, brethren, seek out from among you seven men of good reputation, full of the Holy Spirit and wisdom, whom we may appoint over this business; but we will give ourselves continually to prayer and to the ministry of the Word." And the saying pleased the whole multitude (Acts 6:1-5).

What can we learn from this incident? Note that the leaders of the church did three wise things:

- They addressed the problem right away. They gave it no opportunity to intensify and split the church apart.
- They appointed trustworthy people to take care of the

(147)

problem. They showed that they saw how serious the issue could become; apparently the Hellenists were Jews who had embraced Greek culture, which automatically set up potential for conflict.

- They did not allow a relatively minor issue (distributing daily food) to disrupt them as they studied and prayed and sought to exercise leadership over the church as a whole.

These leaders, probably headed by Peter, distinguished the important from the small. They concentrated on readying themselves to go into the whole world to complete the commission Jesus had given them.

Paul and Petty Problems

When Paul wrote letters to his converts, he usually referred to problems existing in specific churches. Those problems ranged from large to small. In the two Corinthian letters he dealt with the major issues of morality and spiritual gifts for example.

But he also advised the Corinthians about eating meat that had been offered to idols—a relatively minor issue which was nevertheless causing disagreements. Apparently some Christians bought the good cuts of meat at a second-hand meat store so to speak (since the idols didn't eat the meat, the heathen had to do *something* with it). Paul quickly and masterfully resolved the debate over whether such a practice was permissible (1 Cor. 8).

On another occasion Paul wrote a letter of appreciation for a gift the Philippians had sent him in prison. In the entire letter he had only one note of rebuke. He addressed a minor problem so that it did not turn into a serious one: "I implore Euodia and I beg Syntyche to be of the same mind in the Lord" (Phil. 4:2).

Apparently two women had differences of opinion. That seems all that Paul refers to, but he wanted to nip the problem before it pervaded the whole church.

When Molehills Become Mountains

What might have happened had Paul ignored the Euodia-Syntyche situation? What if he had said to himself, "I'll save that for a different letter"? Those two women could have polarized the church by setting brothers and sisters against each other.

I know of a church where just such a tragedy happened. Two women of outstanding ability rose to near-leadership in the women's activities of this church. When the number one women's leader moved away, rivalry broke out. The previous leader had been able to keep the two women separated, busy, and harmoniously working together.

As the two women now vied for leadership, neither seemed to think of herself as doing anything unbiblical or unchristian. But the differences between the two grew until the church was marked by a definite division. Finally people chose sides. Each woman measured her power according to where people sat in worship; all those in one group sat on the left side, the others on the right. A handful of neutrals grouped in the rear of the building, away from everyone else.

Had the pastor been a stronger leader, he might have resolved the problem. But he tried to ignore it for a long time. When that didn't work, he tried to appease both sides. Then both sides ganged up on him and asked for his resignation.

When a new minister came, he unwisely threw his support on one side and the church split. Those who left joined a church two blocks down the street. For years afterward in most of his sermons the pastor attacked those who left. "They have swerved from godliness. They have gone into lesser light," he said.

Wouldn't it have been better for God's kingdom if the first pastor had been able to bring harmony to the two women in the early days of their rivalry? It would have saved so much havoc, pain, and bitterness had that first pastor understood a simple principle:

PRINCIPLE 16:
WISE LEADERS KEEP PETTY PROBLEMS FROM BECOMING MAJOR PROBLEMS.

---

5 Part

THE FUTURE
OF LEADERSHIP

CHAPTER SEVENTEEN

WHERE LEADERS COME FROM

I wonder sometimes about those original twelve disciples. Did Jesus choose them because they had leadership potential, then develop it? Or did He pick a dozen "marginal" men and impart special abilities to them? After the Day of Pentecost, all took on new bravery and eloquence they hadn't shown before; but what did they have in the beginning?

I don't know the answer. But my guess is that the disciples had some leadership qualities before Jesus called them. Andrew, for example, immediately recruited his own brother after meeting Jesus—which shows potential. Peter quickly emerges as a man with a lively mind, a fast tongue, and occasional spiritual insight. In both cases the Lord turned even their weaknesses into strengths.

By contrast, we find discouragement in business and the church when we talk about leadership. Excuses hit us all the time. Too often leaders moan, "I can't find anyone in my church (organization, company, club, or Sunday School) to take responsibility."

Two things bother me about that statement. First, it indicates that leaders are not looking for new leaders in the right places. Second, it tells me that they may be applying the wrong criteria in their search. Let's examine these two ideas.

Looking in the Wrong Places

Some leadership experts estimate that only about 10 percent of any group will show leadership qualities. Chuck Olsen, an authority on small groups and church leadership, traveled extensively among churches in the 1960s and '70s. He observed more than 1,000 congregations in the major denominations and concluded:

No matter how large a congregation becomes, the leadership base stays at approximately sixty-five or seventy people.

He did not *advocate* that as a principle; he did not *like* it; he urged leaders to work to *change* it. But it was the reality, he said.

Most of us look for leadership among those who have already risen to responsible positions. We accept the saying, "If you want something done, ask a busy person." That often works—for awhile. In many organizations, however—especially voluntary ones like the church—we ask, push, pull, beg, and beseech those willing workers until we burn them out. Then they resign, render indifferent service, or learn to pull out endless excuses about why they can't take on any more. Sometimes they just leave us and join *other* groups.

Looking with the Right Perspective

People all around us have latent leadership talents which we can develop. But we usually wait for the emergence of proven leaders instead—to our detriment.

Consider Jesus and His disciples again. At the first mention of the disciples in the Gospels, we don't see much ability in most of them. Levi (Matthew) may have shown more initiative than the others because he collected taxes. Peter, James, and John, on the other hand, earned their livings from fishing. Had they been astute managers, perhaps they would have owned a fleet of boats.

In other words, we know little about the disciples' backgrounds in leadership. Maybe the Gospel writers felt it unimportant to record such information; one significant biblical concept after all, is that we don't dwell on what we were—but what we become. And all those men, trained by Jesus, became leaders.

Discovering Leadership

Jesus did not wait for leadership to present itself. He did not administer tests, inventories, or ask the disciples to write resumés. But with His infallible insight He saw the potential in each of them. He chose them and said, "Come, follow Me."

Too often leaders don't realize that in every congregation or other group, there are enough people to meet the leadership needs. Here's an example from a suburban church.

W.A. and Edna Hanson both stood out as leaders. Their church, like most, had one member who was recognized as the single most powerful person. That was W.A. Meanwhile, Edna took responsibility in every activity involving women. Together the Hansons carried the bulk of the congregations' leadership; if anything needed doing, the pastor or members had only to call W.A. or Edna and it got done.

Then a shock wave hit: The Hansons had to move. Edna had developed health problems; her doctor said that only by moving to a warmer climate could she hope to find relief.

After two years of suffering through cold winters, the couple moved to sunny Florida.

Even before they left, the church mourned their loss. The pastor, perhaps more than anyone else, saw the vacuum they would leave behind. *What will we do?* he asked himself over and over.

Two weeks before W.A. and Edna left, the pastor made an appeal from the pulpit: "We have a number of jobs that W.A. and Edna have been doing here. We need folks who are willing to fill in the gap and take over their responsibilities."

To his surprise, people responded. By the time the Hansons left, eight people had moved into leadership roles to take over the jobs W.A. and Edna had done. The pastor would speak many times of the following valuable lessons he learned from that experience:

1. No one is indispensable in the work of God's kingdom.
2. People may not recognize their own leadership abilities until someone discovers them and gives them opportunities.
3. Leadership emerges when people receive opportunities to develop themselves.
4. People emerge into leadership positions when they know they are wanted.
5. Most leaders learn on the job.

On-the-Job Leadership Training

Jesus taught His disciples didactically and by His own example. He pointed to the future, when they would be on their own without Him. Eventually He commissioned them: "As the Father has sent Me, I also send you" (John 20:21).

His leaving meant they had to fall back on their training,

native abilities, and access to the Holy Spirit for guidance. They found themselves having to lead or leave.

On the Day of Pentecost, for instance, crowds gathered around them after the arrival of the Holy Spirit. "What's going on?" people asked. Peter rose to the occasion and preached one of the greatest sermons in history.

A few days later the elders and chief priests commanded them not to preach anymore, but they did anyway. When brought to the tribunal, Peter and John said "Whether it is right in the sight of God to listen to you more than to God, you judge. For we cannot but speak the things which we have seen and heard" (Acts 4:19-20).

Example after example of the disciples' boldness explodes in the Book of Acts. The fruition of leadership took place three years after Jesus said to them, "Follow Me."

Scripture and tradition give us a partial picture of what happened to the apostles: Herod killed James the brother of John; Peter's great ministry continued; Thomas apparently became the apostle to India and the Far East. Young Mark founded the Coptic Church, the Church of Alexandria which was later in the forefront of Christianity for 200 years. The other apostles also traveled the known world and proclaimed the Gospel.

To many people of that day, the disciples must have appeared an unlikely group for God to use. But Jesus saw something special in them—and developed that "something" through on-the-job training.

Knowing People

Probably no quality helps more in choosing and developing leaders than that elusive one we sometimes call *intuition* or *insight*. Jesus proved His powers of insight with statements like this one, made in the Upper Room after He had washed the disciples' feet: " 'He who is bathed needs only to wash his feet, but is completely clean; and you are clean, but not all of you.' For He knew who would betray Him; therefore He said, 'You are not all clean' " (John 13:10-11).

Jesus knew people's inner selves—both the good and the evil (John 2:23-25). He knew Judas and the evil of his heart; He knew John and James and Nathanael and saw their leadership potentials.

How to Choose Leaders

Where and how can we find new leaders? Here are several suggestions based on biblical principles:

1. *Choose the faithful.* In Jesus' Parable of the Talents, the master praised his most profitable servant as follows: "Well done, good and faithful servant; you have been faithful over a few things, I will make you ruler over many things" (Matt. 25:23). In other words, he who is faithful in little will be faithful in much.

Find those who consistently do the small "backstage" jobs. Their spheres of responsibility may be as limited as keeping classroom attendance, making coffee every Sunday, or helping others when time allows. When these folks find themselves recognized for the little jobs they do faithfully, they may be willing to increase their responsibilities. Every time they try a new task and do it well, they are propelled one step closer toward leadership.

2. *Pray for wisdom.* That may seem obvious, but I find that when leaders need recruits, they start by asking, "Who would be willing to do it? Who won't turn us down?" They don't start by talking with God.

I know a church whose pastor and Sunday School superintendent were suddenly faced with a fearsome statistic. Over half their twenty-one teachers planned to give up their classes before the September quarter began. It was the first of May when they learned this, and they reacted with panic. They tried to think of people they could beg or coerce into teaching.

Then one of them said, "Let's pray before we go wild over all this." So they prayed—and agreed to keep praying for two days before meeting again. Two days later their sense of panic had gone. They devised a plan to look for people with teaching *potential*. By June, they had their full complement of teachers for fall! They'd learned a valuable lesson too.

3. *Remember that there are no "no-talent" people.* Many churches today, suddenly aware of the concept of spiritual gifts (Rom. 12:3-8; 1 Cor. 12; 14; Eph. 4:7-16), have been learning how to put them into practice. A number of leaders have found that it works to proceed on the premise that no church has members who are without talent.

In whatever way they do it, the point is not only to get the church's work done: it is also to help Christians identify and use the abilities God has given them. As one pastor said during a sermon on spiritual gifts, "Use it or lose it."

One church appointed a committee of ten resourceful, imaginative individuals. The ten divided up the church roster and visited members in their homes or work places, talking with them about their spiritual talents. They allowed no one to get away with saying, "I think God passed me by."

Those ten wanted to encourage members not only to discover but to *use* their God-given abilities. As one member said, "If each church really is a body, no wonder many of them have problems! How can you have a body functioning at 100 percent when you're missing a leg or an eye or even small parts like elbow joints or kneecaps? When all members of a body fulfill their tasks, it operates perfectly and beautifully."

4. *Affirm the leaders you choose.* We have no record of

Jesus coming around every day and complimenting the disciples on their leadership qualities. But we do know He affirmed those who lived righteously. He told them that with one exception they were clean (John 13:10). On His last night with them before His arrest, He said,

> You are My friends if you do whatever I command you. No longer do I call you servants, for a servant does not know what his master is doing; but I have called you friends, for all things that I have heard from My Father I have made known to you (John 15:14-15).

After His resurrection Jesus commissioned His workers. (John 20:21). In His final discussion with the disciples, according to John's Gospel, He affirmed Peter's ministry despite the latter's previous denial of Jesus. Christ asked Peter three times, "Do you love Me?" Each time He added a command: "Feed My lambs" (John 21:15); "Tend My sheep" (v. 16); and finally, "Feed My sheep" (v. 17).

Only by reading the ongoing story in Acts can we see how vastly the disciples' leadership developed. God used them to change the world. Perhaps more than anything else, that shows that Jesus' way of choosing and teaching His leaders *works*.

PRINCIPLE 17:
LEADERS ARE CHOSEN AND EQUIPPED BY GOD; WE HAVE BUT TO DISCOVER AND DEVELOP THEM.

CHAPTER EIGHTEEN

TURNING FOLLOWERS INTO LEADERS

I recently studied John 13—17 because I wanted to think about the last words Jesus spoke to His disciples before His arrest. What He said was more than a farewell; it was a summary of their three-year apprenticeship with Him. For a long time He had been telling them gently that they would soon be on their own. Now He promised to send them a Helper, the Holy Spirit.

It must have been difficult for those followers to understand Jesus' words. Much of what He said could only be grasped later. Perhaps it was hard for Jesus too. He had worked with the disciples, taught them, and lived His commitment before them day after day. Soon they would have to go on without His physical presence.

But the disciples went on to succeed. Today we can look at Jesus' leadership style and thank Him for it. He pushed His followers forward without waiting for them to demand responsibility, position, or office.

By contrast, I've known of many leader-follower relationships that started well and went sour. In one instance, a fine, committed elder named Charles chose a young convert named David and said, "I would like to work with you and train you for responsible leadership in our church." The younger man agreed.

The elder took David with him while visiting the sick in the hospital, making evangelistic calls, or doing anything he felt would help the younger Christian grow. Charles taught a large Sunday School class and worked patiently with David to develop his teaching abilities. In the process the two men became as close as any father and son.

Sounds good, doesn't it? It was, for about three years. Eventually David wanted to do things on his own. He wanted to think for himself, to make his own decisions about his ministry in the congregation. Charles had taught him well, and he felt he needed to put his teaching skill into practice. At the same time he felt shy about visiting prospects and did not believe he should try to concentrate in that area.

A rift developed when Charles balked at allowing David to make his own choices. He had been directing David's life and didn't want to give it up—though he would never have admitted it. Eventually David left that church, joined another, and soon rose to a position of leadership.

Charles was hurt. He felt the man he'd trained had let him down. Too bad he didn't understand our final principle from the life of Jesus:

PRINCIPLE 18:
LEADERS DISCIPLE OTHERS
WHO BECOME LEADERS
WHO DISCIPLE OTHERS.

Preparing Others to Take Over

One characteristic of good leaders is that they prepare others to take over. They don't just prepare their followers to "do well," but prepare them to do everything they are doing themselves. These successors may not always measure up; they may not fit the roles prepared for them; or they may even outshine their mentors.

Jesus worked toward this end with His handful of recruits—teaching, training, rebuking, building, and showing them the way. He made this significant statement to them: "Most assuredly, I say to you, he who believes in Me, the works that I do he will do also; and greater works than these he will do, because I go to My Father" (John 14:12). That's part of the preparing principle—teaching followers to outdo their master.

Years ago I heard a Christian speaker lay down the following two leader-forming principles:

1. *Give others responsibility before they're ready for it.* He didn't imply that we should carelessly shove people into higher positions. He meant that the best way to train others is to make them stretch. Just *before* they're ready to fill a job, give it to them. Make the job bigger than they are. Then they must keep on growing to measure up.

2. *Give potential leaders everything before they ask for it.* He explained it another way: We hold on by letting go. If the leader hangs on until he feels the follower is ready to take over, the follower may *demand* the position. That tends to put everyone on the defensive. Why not prepare followers to take over even before they know they want to?

Transitions work that way in business, church, and family. Passing on responsibility takes careful planning.

One Christian organization's leaders, for example, prefer to promote from within. They seldom go outside the company unless they cannot find qualified inside people who can be trained to fit a position. They have seldom had to go beyond their own organization. As a result, employees of that company know their supervisors recognize potential in everyone.

The Replacement Principle

A pastor retired after twenty-nine years of leading three thriving churches. In each church attendance had at least doubled during his years there. To mark his retirement, friends and converts from throughout his ministry arranged a special dinner.

Just before the pastor gave his final sermon, one of his former associates asked, "As you leave the active ministry and look back, what do you consider the single best thing, you accomplished?"

The older man thought for a second. Then his face lit up. "That's an easy one," he said. "The thirty-seven people who are in some form of Christian ministry today—I had the great privilege of being their pastor."

He didn't tell his assembled friends how much he had done to encourage those thirty-seven people. But the fact was that he had wisely waited until they showed initiative or started to talk to him about greater service. Once such people opened the door and showed their desire to serve Jesus Christ more fully, that pastor encouraged them each step of the way.

At one time, for instance, four members of the pastor's congregation were in school preparing for the ordained ministry. He not only encouraged them to speak in public, but actually arranged the worship services so they could participate. At first, they did simple things like making announcements or reading Scriptures. As they became accustomed to speaking in front of people, the pastor arranged opportunities for them to lead another church's midweek service or preach when a local pastor went on vacation. The pastor himself had four Sundays away from the pulpit each year, and arranged for his students-in-training to preach on these days.

This is a biblical principle. In the Old Testament, Joshua studied under Moses. When God took Moses home, Joshua became the leader. Elijah had a great ministry in the Northern Kingdom; after his translation into heaven, Elisha became the foremost prophet of Israel.

In the New Testament, Paul constantly trained others. He always took along several men when he went on his missionary trips. John Mark, Barnabas' nephew, left in the middle of the first missionary journey, but later became more responsible. Paul wrote to Timothy, "Get Mark and bring him with you, for he is useful to me for ministry" (2 Tim. 4:11). Others, like Demas (2 Tim. 4:10), later chose to go their own ways.

It appears that Paul discipled Priscilla and Aquila (Acts 18:2, 26), and that they discipled Apollos (Acts 18:24-28). That's the real meaning of discipleship—teaching followers so that, in time, they may teach others. As Paul wrote to Timothy, "And the things that you have heard from me among many witnesses, commit these to faithful men who will be able to teach others also" (2 Tim. 2:2).

That's how the Gospel is perpetuated. That is also how leadership should be relayed in business, the church, and the family.

Training the Runners
Jesus used at least four methods to train His followers to become leaders. These methods can be used to prepare leaders in any field:

1. *Teaching Precepts.* This is what most of us think of as training—offering principles, knowledge. In the Old Testament, Eli used this method with Samuel. After coming to the temple as a child, Samuel grew under the leadership of Eli. Through the years Eli taught him the role of being a priest—what a priest had to do, wear, and say. The day came when Samuel took on the responsibility of being high priest to the Jewish nation.

2. *Showing by example.* Students pick up at least as much from the characters and lifestyles of their teachers as they do from their spoken words. In fact, many educators would say that the personhood of the teacher communicates far more than anything else.

A century ago Brooks Phillips defined preaching as "truth through personality." I believe he would agree that truth is truth, no matter who says it. But truth also comes clothed in the personality of the messenger. The individual giving the instruction says as much by appearance, personality, and attitude as by receiving the material itself.

In the 1960s Marshall McLuhan said much the same thing when he told the world, "The medium is the message." Just as we can tell a hypocrite, "Your actions speak so loudly I can't hear a word you're saying," we can say to a consistent teacher, "Your life speaks so positively, I hear everything you're telling me."

Jesus was consistent. Nowhere do the Gospel writers suggest that the disciples questioned the sincerity or integrity of Jesus, even though they questioned nearly everything else. Consistency is basic to being a model for leaders-to-be.

3. *Demonstrating by results.* When Jesus talked with His critics, He asked them to believe in Him. Then He said, "If you can't believe Me, then believe Me because of the works I do" (John 10:38, author's paraphrase). One time He said, "The works which the Father has given Me to finish—the

very works that I do—bear witness of Me, that the Father has sent Me" (5:36).

4. *Pointing to the witness of others.* Jesus referred to John the Baptist as a witness of His ministry. Paul, in listing the qualifications of a bishop or overseer, said, "Moreover he must have a good testimony among those who are outside, lest he fall into reproach and the snare of the devil" (1 Tim. 3:7).

Yes, even the testimony of non-Christians can help us grow toward leadership. We need to remind ourselves that those outside the faith often watch God's people closely— sometimes with a tendency to condemn. If God's leaders in business, school, and the church sincerely live the Christian faith, unbelievers (sometimes grudgingly) acknowledge the faithfulness of those leaders.

A pastor friend was reminded of that when the new editor of a suburban weekly paper came to see him.

"I wanted to interview two people" the editor said. "So I began asking, 'Who is the most influential preacher in the county?' Almost everybody gave me your name. I was preparing for a second interview, so I asked another question: 'If you had only one person to trust outside your close friends and relatives, who in the county would you consider going to?' Almost everybody gave me your name on that one too."

When I heard that story, I thought of the impact of that leader's life and commitment on his community. Long after he's gone, the results of his ministry will remain. He has prepared others by teaching and by living what he taught. The truth of what he's taught has been validated by results and the testimonies of Christians and non-Christians alike.

What better legacy could any leader hope to leave his followers?

THE LEADERSHIP STYLE OF JESUS

Congratulations, Graduates!

Every course of instruction must one day come to an end. Students receive their diplomas, degrees, or leaving certificates. Eventually they must go out and get on the job. They have completed their preparation.

If there was such a thing as a graduation ceremony for the first disciples, it occurred in John 20:19-23. After the Resurrection, Jesus appeared to His followers in the same Upper Room in which they had eaten the Passover meal together. He said these words to them: "As the Father has sent Me, I also send you" (v. 21). The preparation had ended. Now they would go into the rest of the world and proclaim the Gospel.

That's the purpose of training others—to make them leaders who will train others who may also become leaders. Jesus started this by multiplying His physical capacity by twelve.

Shouldn't that be the goal of *our* leadership styles as well?